Mediterranean
Every Day

Brimming with creative inspiration, how-to projects, and useful information to enrich your everyday life, Quarto Knows is a favorite destination for those pursuing their interests and passions. Visit our site and dig deeper with our books into your area of interest: Quarto Creates, Quarto Cooks, Quarto Homes, Quarto Lives, Quarto Drives, Quarto Explores, Quarto Gifts, or Quarto Kids.

First Published in 2020 by The Harvard Common Press, an imprint of The Quarto Group, 100 Cummings Center, Suite 265-D, Beverly, MA 01915, USA.
T (978) 282-9590 F (978) 283-2742 QuartoKnows.com

The Harvard Common Press titles are also available at discount for retail, wholesale, promotional, and bulk purchase. For details, contact the Special Sales Manager by email at specialsales@quarto.com or by mail at The Quarto Group, Attn: Special Sales Manager, 100 Cummings Center, Suite 265-D, Beverly, MA 01915, USA.

24 23 22 21   4 5

ISBN: 978-1-55832-999-7

Digital edition published in 2020
eISBN: 978-1-59233-945-7

Library of Congress Cataloging-in-Publication Data

Names: Prakash, Sheela, author.
Title: Mediterranean every day : simple, inspired recipes for feel-good
  food / Sheela Prakash.
Description: Beverly, MA : Harvard Common Press, 2020. | Includes index.
Identifiers: LCCN 2020010626 (print) | LCCN 2020010627 (ebook) | ISBN
  9781558329997 (paperback) | ISBN 9781592339457 (ebook)
Subjects: LCSH: Cooking, Mediterranean. | LCGFT: Cookbooks.
Classification: LCC TX725 .P754 2020 (print) | LCC TX725 (ebook) | DDC
  641.59/1822--dc23
LC record available at https://lccn.loc.gov/2020010626
LC ebook record available at https://lccn.loc.gov/2020010627

Design: Timothy Samara
Photography: Kristin Teig Photography
Food Stylist: Catrine Kelty

Printed in China

Mediterranean Every Day

Simple, Inspired Recipes for Feel-Good Food

SHEELA PRAKASH

HARVARD
COMMON
PRESS

Contents

9 *Introduction*

11 WHERE TO BEGIN

12 About the Mediterranean Diet

12 From Diet to Casual Mediterranean-Style Cooking

15 Pantry Staples

19 Pantry Enhancers

    20 Any Herb Pesto

    23 Freezer Bread Crumbs

    25 Salsa Verde

    27 Everyday Vinaigrette

    28 Herb-Infused Honey

    28 Spicy Chili Oil

    30 Roasted Garlic

33 THREE-INGREDIENT (OR FEWER) SNACKS AND COCKTAILS

34 Herby Ricotta

36 Za'atar Pistachios

39 Roasted Garlic–Marinated Olives

41 Slinky Red Peppers with Capers and Sherry Vinegar

42 Cacio e Pepe Farinata

45 Smoky White Bean Hummus

47 Fennel and Parmesan "Crostini"

48 Fig in a Pig

50 Honeyed Prosecco

51 Americano

52 Limonata Smash

55 Cocchi Americano Spritz

57 SALADS AND SOUPS

58 Asparagus Salad with Radishes, Snap Peas, and Avocado

61 Mixed Melon and Prosciutto Caprese

63 Mediterranean Niçoise Salad

65 Peak-Summer Panzanella

68 Hot Smoked Salmon Greek Salad

71 Warm Roasted Delicata Squash and Kale Salad

72 The Easiest Arugula Salad

73 Roasted Greek Tomato Soup

74 Cucumber Tahini Gazpacho with Crispy Spiced Chickpeas

76 Spicy Sausage and Rice Soup

79 Garlic Parmesan Soup with Greens and Beans

83 BEANS, GRAINS, AND A FEW BREADY THINGS

84 Olive Oil–Braised White Beans

87 Black Lentil Fritters with Lemon-Herb Yogurt

89 Spicy Broccoli Rabe and Chickpea Skillet

90 Chickpea Flatbread with Whipped Feta and Marinated Tomatoes

93 Cheesy Brussels Sprout and Farro Bake

96 No-Fail Parmesan Risotto

    99 Summer: Fresh Corn and Cherry Tomato Risotto

    100 Fall: Sweet Potato and Sage Risotto

    101 Winter: Mushroom and Radicchio Risotto

    103 Spring: Lemony Asparagus Risotto

105 Creamy Oven Polenta

    106 Quick Sausage Ragù over Polenta

    107 Shrimp Scampi over Polenta

    108 White Bean Ratatouille over Polenta

111 Whole-Wheat Skillet Focaccia

113 Mozzarella Anchovy Toast

114 Tomato Bread with Burrata and Salsa Verde

117 COLORFUL PASTAS

119 Bucatini Aglio e Olio with Wilted Arugula

120 No-Cook Summer Tomato Pasta

123 Orzo Skillet with Shrimp and Feta

125 Caramelized Mushroom Pasta with Crispy Prosciutto

127 Lemony Yogurt and Zucchini Linguine

128 Spaghetti and Meatball Ragù

131 Balsamic Brown Butter Tortellini with Spinach and Hazelnuts

134 Pasta with Burst Cherry Tomatoes and Swordfish

137 Pesto Pasta with Charred Radicchio

139 Melted Broccoli Pasta with Capers and Anchovies

141 Israeli Couscous Salad with Herbs, Green Olives, and Pistachios

144 Baked Spinach Artichoke Gnudi

147 GATHERING DISHES

148 Thyme Pesto Roast Chicken with Crispy Potatoes

151 Salmon in Crazy Water

153 Caramelized Leek and Fennel Galette with Blue Cheese

155 Flank Steak Tagliata with Arugula and Parmesan

158 Broiled Swordfish with Fennel-Caper Slaw

161 Braised Harissa Eggplant and Greens

162 Sausage, Pepper, and Onion Oven Bake

163 Rosemary Brown Butter Scallops

164 Skillet Lemon Chicken Thighs with Blistered Olives

166 Roasted Cod Saltimbocca

169 Crispy Spiced Lamb and Cauliflower with Dates

170 Baked Chicken Milanese with Lemony Escarole

172 Mussels all'Amatriciana

175 Shawarma-Spiced Halloumi and Vegetables

177 Eggs in Purgatory

178 Broccoli Steaks with Walnut-Raisin Salsa

181 DESSERTS

182 Chocolate Olive Oil Cake

185 Rosé-Soaked Peaches

186 London Fog Affogato

188 Apricot Almond Clafoutis

190 Tahini Truffles

193 Raspberry Ricotta Gratin

194 Citrus Polenta Cake

197 Chocolate Pear Crumble

199 Greek Yogurt Panna Cotta

202 Roasted Figs with Dark Chocolate and Sea Salt

203 *Resources*

204 *Acknowledgments*

205 *About the Author*

206 *Index*

Introduction

When I think about what or who inspired my deep affection for Mediterranean cuisine, it's a simple answer: Graziella. Picture the most Italian of Italian nonne—*a bit rotund, apple-cheeked, with an apron almost always tied around her waist. I'd lived in Italy and had traveled around the Mediterranean and tasted great food—some of the best ever—before I met Graziella, but it wasn't until her that I knew what true Mediterranean food was—that it's a feeling more than a practice.*

A few days after I graduated college, I packed up my miniscule studio apartment in Greenwich Village and flew to Italy. I'd studied in Florence my junior year, and the moment I left, I knew I had to return. So soon after, I applied and was accepted for a post-graduate summer internship on an idyllic farm, *Tenuta di Spannocchia*, south of Florence near the medieval town of Siena. There were eight of us, from all corners of the world, and we all were given specific roles on the farm—I was assigned the *orto*, or vegetable garden.

Each day I weeded, planted, and harvested, and in the evenings I'd head into the kitchen. As an *agriturismo*, the farm held dinner every night for its guests and Graziella was the cook. She was stubborn, re-lentless, and quickly became my most favorite person on the farm. Graziella didn't understand or speak a lick of English (or so she said), and yet, with my very broken Italian, we had a wonderful understanding. I'd come into the kitchen each evening to help her prepare the meal. That might have meant I'd stand over the pot of risotto and stir, or simply give her company while she threw together whatever vegetables I had harvested that day into a salad. She taught me that Mediterranean food is so much more casual and relaxed than the great cookbooks and restaurants tell you. Understand the true attitude behind it and you've unlocked the secret. What is that attitude? Be ridiculously unfussy.

When I returned to the States, I brought this attitude with me. Slowly but surely it became the only way I knew how to cook. My meals were inspired by my time with Graziella: They'd honor the flavors, traditions, and overall wholesomeness of Mediterranean cuisine but be adapted depending on what happened to be in my refrigerator, the limited equipment in my tiny kitchen, how much time I had, and honestly, how motivated I really was to churn out a meal.

What made me fall in love with the food of the Mediterranean—and I think, really, what has made the entire world fall and continue to fall in love with it—is its uncomplicated nature, which is exactly what this book is about.

CHAPTER 1

Where to Begin

This book harnesses the relaxed attitude of Mediterranean cooking. Each recipe isn't made to feel overwhelming or time consuming and most (though there are a few exceptions) are easy enough to pull off no matter the night of the week. This is the type of food I cook each and every night, whether just for my husband, Joe, and me or when family or friends gather around the table with us. The flavors of the Mediterranean—the grassy olive oil, the sweet tomatoes, the fragrant herbs—are what most inspire me and also just so happen to be ingredients that naturally lend themselves to wholesome, satisfying eating.

Feel confident in your abilities as a home cook, no matter your skill level, and approach these recipes with your own intuition. I hope to be a friend in the kitchen as you cook through the recipes, urging you to trust yourself, rather than someone calling to you from the pages to overcomplicate things. With this outlook, there's no doubt that what comes out of your kitchen will be delicious.

About the Mediterranean Diet

Diets come and go more quickly than I can keep up with them, which has never actually bothered me because I don't believe in any of them. As a registered dietitian, I am constantly asked for advice on how to eat or how to achieve particular health goals, and my answer is always the same: everything in moderation. Which, depending on the person, is not always well received because we live in a society that desires quick fixes. Luckily, however, there is one diet I look toward to prove my point—the Mediterranean diet.

The Mediterranean diet isn't a diet in the traditional sense, though. Instead, it's a way of eating that's been done for centuries in countries that surround the Mediterranean Sea. Each cuisine is unique, of course—Greek food is not Italian food, nor is it Spanish food—and within each country there are wide variations, but there are pillars that remain true throughout. Most importantly, nothing is off the table. Instead, the focus is on heart-healthy ingredients such as olive oil, fatty fish, and nuts, along with vegetables, fruits, and whole grains. Dairy, red meat, and sweets are hardly forbidden and instead enjoyed in moderation, as is wine. I am not the first person to reveal the diet's health benefits: It's been well researched and publicized that eating this way reduces your risk of a multitude of chronic diseases and aids in weight management and overall well-being.

Most importantly, it's a lifelong way to eat. We're on this planet for such a brief time that I've never understood the point in depriving oneself. I do understand eating to feel your best, though, which is what the Mediterranean diet is all about.

From Diet to Casual Mediterranean-Style Cooking

It's important that I make this very clear: This isn't a diet book. Remember how I said I don't believe in diets?

Everything I learned from my time living abroad revealed that cooking in this healthful manner can come quite naturally, if you let it. The Mediterranean diet is a style of cooking and eating more than anything else. It celebrates the diverse flavors of the cuisine while embracing a relaxed, flexible attitude. It's about creating meals simple enough for midweek but never out of place for a weekend gathering with friends. It's about leaning on feel-good, colorful ingredients, such as fresh vegetables and fruits, spices, and herbs, to drive your meals. It's also about using what you have on hand to limit waste in the kitchen, which means it's just as much about seasonality and well-rounded eating as it is about leaning on the pantry.

The recipes in this book are a practice in this unfussy manner of cooking. My hope is that you cook and enjoy them, of course, but with each recipe comes a greater purpose: that you walk away with a better understanding of this style of cooking. That, in turn, you gain the confidence to step away from the recipes and begin to play around and improvise in an attempt to create simple, wholesome meals more intuitively. Try different cheeses and herbs in pesto to see how they affect flavor, add a sprinkle of toasted nuts to a salad to lend texture, or toss extra vegetables into your pasta if you discover some in the crisper drawer that are starting to look past their prime. Most importantly, though, just have fun. If you do, then this kind of cooking comes easily.

Pantry Staples

A well-stocked pantry is the true lifeline of the kitchen. This is the case no matter the cuisine—Mediterranean or otherwise. Keep a collection of wholesome ingredients on hand at all times and you'll always have the ability to throw together an unfussy meal, without having to make frequent runs to the grocery store.

When I say pantry, though, I don't simply mean dry goods—refrigerator and freezer staples are just as much a part of the equation. Also, because I am a minimalist at heart, I believe less equals more. An overflowing pantry doesn't equate to better (or easier) meals. Instead, invest in a handful of ingredients that affirm their shelf space plus some, rather than being such an occasional reach that they soon start collecting dust. Here are the staple Mediterranean ingredients to stock in your pantry.

Oils and Vinegars

Extra-virgin olive oil I like to keep two bottles on hand: one quality grocery store extra-virgin olive oil to cook with (my choice is California Olive Ranch) and a fancier bottle to use for finishing dishes like soups and salads, to dunk bread into, or even to drizzle on vanilla ice cream.

Balsamic vinegar More sweet and savory than tangy, balsamic can be used for a whole lot more than just salad dressings. In the Quick Sausage Ragù over Polenta (page 106), it provides depth of flavor without slow simmering.

Red wine vinegar A crowd-pleasing vinegar that's perfect in vinaigrettes (see Everyday Vinaigrette, page 27) and condiments (see Salsa Verde, page 25).

Sherry vinegar A touch less essential than the preceding two vinegars, but once you make room for a bottle in your pantry, I doubt you'll ever look back. It's somewhere between red wine vinegar and balsamic vinegar, in terms of body, and delivers a slightly nutty, complex flavor that makes everything it touches fancier.

Seasonings and Aromatics

Kosher salt All recipes in this book are developed using Diamond Crystal kosher salt, the gold standard among many home and professional cooks. It's the brand I recommend because most recipes, even aside from the ones in this book, are developed using it. Morton's, the other popular brand of kosher salt, is saltier, so if you use it instead, using the same amount of salt noted in a recipe, you might find you've oversalted your dish. My best advice, if using another brand or another type of salt entirely, is to use a light hand and taste as you go.

Flaky sea salt I keep a jar of Maldon sea salt flakes right next to the kosher salt on my kitchen counter and reach for it almost as frequently. It's strictly a finishing salt: Sprinkle a pinch or two on salads, soups, and even your favorite chocolate chip cookies before baking to add a touch of salty crunch.

Freshly ground black pepper Rather than using the pre-ground stuff, I prefer to grind black peppercorns straight from a pepper mill to achieve the best flavor.

Red pepper flakes They're not just for sprinkling on pizza. Red pepper flakes add the perfect amount of heat to pasta dishes, sauces, and more.

Garlic I tend to buy at least two heads at a time: one for roasting (see Roasted Garlic, page 30) and one for using in just about every meal I make.

Shallots Compared to onions, shallots have a mellower flavor that's a touch sweet and garlicky, so I find them extremely versatile. They work well cooked and raw and can be used in place of onions in a pinch.

Pasta and Grains

Dried pasta Keep one long shape, such as spaghetti, and one short shape, such as penne, stocked for easy dinners.

Farro I love the chewy, toothsome texture whole-grain farro has, and I often substitute it for quinoa or rice. It makes a starring appearance in the Cheesy Brussels Sprout and Farro Bake (page 93).

Polenta A bag of course-ground polenta is a great base for a comforting dinner (see Creamy Oven Polenta, page 105). I also love to bake with it for its texture and flavor (see Citrus Polenta Cake, page 194).

Risotto rice Once you realize just how easy risotto is to make (see No-Fail Parmesan Risotto, page 96), you'll understand why short-grain Italian rice, such as carnaroli or arborio, is a staple.

Canned and Jarred Goods

Anchovies Trust me on this one: If you're anchovy averse, know that one or two can boost a dish's flavor tenfold. Most of the time, because they dissolve when cooked, you won't even know they're there. Opt for tins or jars packed in olive oil.

Beans I keep both dried and canned beans stocked in my pantry, but, for everyday purposes, I tend to reach for the cans more frequently. Keep a couple of your favorite types around—for me that's chickpeas and cannellini beans—for quick meals. You'll find even simply braising them in the oven slowly with good olive oil and aromatics can transform them (see Olive Oil–Braised White Beans, page 84).

Capers Keep what you can find on hand, but I do think it's worth seeking out salt-packed capers. They have a more refined flavor than those packed in vinegar brine, which end up tasting more like vinegar. Just rinse salt-packed capers well in a small fine-mesh strainer before using, to wash away the salt.

Dijon mustard This is such a staple for me that I always have a backup jar ready to go when I run out. It adds the perfect tang and depth of flavor to everything from salad dressings to casseroles. If I've picked up salmon fillets or some chicken with no set plan, I usually find a swipe of Dijon before baking does the trick. After trying just about every brand, Maille is my favorite.

Good marinara sauce For the times I am feeling lazy, a jar of good marinara sauce and a box of dried pasta can be a lifesaver. Rao's is more expensive than other common brands but, once you try it, you'll understand why.

Tahini I always thought tahini was chalky and bitter until I tasted the tahini made by the brand Soom. Now I use it to add nutty richness to everything from soup (see Cucumber Tahini Gazpacho, page 74), skillet dinners (see Crispy Spiced Lamb and Cauliflower with Dates, page 169), and even dessert (see Tahini Truffles, page 190).

Whole peeled tomatoes My go-to brand is Cento but any brand you like the taste of is a good choice. Whole tomatoes can easily be used as they are or diced or crushed into bite-size pieces, so I find it easier to keep only them stocked rather than a wide variety of cans—plus, I think their flavor is better.

Flours and Baking Supplies

All-purpose flour You probably already have it, but it's worth calling out this baking basic. Choose unbleached all-purpose flour, such as the one from King Arthur Flour, which is my go-to brand.

Almond flour Not to be confused with almond meal, almond flour has a fine texture that produces moist, richly flavored baked goods. Try it in the Citrus Polenta Cake (page 194) and you'll see what I mean. It's naturally gluten-free.

Chickpea flour This high-protein, naturally gluten-free flour is best in savory applications, as it has a nutty flavor likened to the bean itself. It's the key ingredient in the Cacio e Pepe Farinata (page 42) and the Chickpea Flatbread with Whipped Feta and Marinated Tomatoes (page 90), as well as the binder for the Black Lentil Fritters with Lemon-Herb Yogurt (page 87).

Cocoa powder and good chocolate Because a chocolate craving can strike at any moment, I like to be prepared. It's wise to keep unsweetened cocoa powder, either Dutch-process or natural, on hand as well as good chocolate (bittersweet or dark, 60 to 70 percent cacao) for baking, though I've been known to simply break off a square or two of the latter to satisfy, too.

Honey Hardly just for baking, honey is my favorite sweetener. I top my morning bowl of yogurt with it, use it in cocktails (see Honeyed Prosecco, page 50), and even like to drizzle a bit on vegetables before roasting to help caramelize them.

Granulated sugar I prefer to use alternative sweeteners when possible, but it's hard to write off white sugar completely when baking. So, I keep it stocked and use it judiciously.

Whole-Wheat Flour When used alone, this whole-grain flour results in something that's quite dense and hearty, which is why I like to blend it with all-purpose flour. Try it in the Whole-Wheat Skillet Focaccia (page 111).

In the Refrigerator

Eggs Add a fried, poached, or boiled egg to just about anything and it becomes a meal. Though a simple scramble, maybe with some greens or leftover roasted vegetables tossed in, is a comforting meal in its own right, if you ask me.

Fresh herbs You don't have to keep a huge variety of fresh herbs on hand, but I like to have at least a bunch of fresh parsley in the fridge to use as a garnish and to add fresh flavor to dishes. Store the bunch with its stems in a glass of water and the leaves loosely covered with a plastic bag and it will keep well for a week or two.

Greek yogurt Whole milk plain Greek yogurt can transition from breakfast bowl to creamy dinner component to dessert dollop seamlessly. The Hot Smoked Salmon Greek Salad (page 68), Lemony Yogurt and Zucchini Linguine (page 127), and Greek Yogurt Panna Cotta (page 199) are just a few recipes in this book that prove it.

Hard cheeses Specifically a chunk of Parmigiano Reggiano (a.k.a. Parmesan) and a chunk of Pecorino Romano to freshly grate over just about everything. The latter is saltier and a bit funkier, which adds flair, but if you only pick one to have at all times, choose Parmesan. Oh, and definitely save the spent Parmesan rinds to make soups (see Garlic Parmesan Soup with Greens and Beans, page 79).

Lemons They last for weeks in the refrigerator and just a squeeze of juice can add incredible brightness to just about anything.

Nuts Whatever the nut, it's best stored in the refrigerator for the longest shelf life. Almonds, hazelnuts, and pistachios are well loved in Mediterranean cooking, though, really, I show no bias.

Olives These are essential because they double as both flavorful ingredient and snack. I like to keep both a jar of deep purple Kalamata and green Castelvetrano olives in the fridge for variety—and always choose unpitted for the best flavor.

In the Freezer

Good bread Keep a thick-sliced loaf of good sourdough bread, or country-style bread, sealed in a large zip-top freezer bag and you've always got a way to round out a meal. Or, turn it into a meal (see Tomato Bread with Burrata and Salsa Verde, page 114).

Pantry Enhancers

Choose not to step beyond pantry basics and you undoubtedly can cook well. In fact, most of the time that's exactly how I keep my kitchen. However, when I am inspired to make Any Herb Pesto (page 20) from the herbs in my tiny (but overflowing) container garden or take a little time to make my own Spicy Chili Oil (page 28), I am never regretful. Consider this chapter Pantry 2.0. Once you've got the staples under your belt, go ahead and have a little fun jazzing up your collections of ingredients. Homemade sauces and condiments are surprisingly easy to pull off and yet can add an entirely new element to a dish—even if it's a dead-simple one. Make a batch of Everyday Vinaigrette (page 27), toss some of it with salad greens, and you'll immediately realize your usual store-bought bottle can never compare.

Any Herb Pesto

2 garlic cloves, crushed

¼ cup (30 g) nuts or seeds, toasted

2 cups (56 g) packed fresh tender herb leaves, or greens

1 ice cube

⅓ cup (80 ml) extra-virgin olive oil

¼ cup packed (14 g) fresh finely grated hard cheese

½ teaspoon fresh lemon juice

Kosher salt

—

Makes about ¾ cup (about 180 g)

Once you start thinking of pesto as an equation rather than a recipe, you'll quickly realize the possibilities are endless. Just about any soft, tender herb or green—like parsley, cilantro, tarragon, spinach, or arugula—will work. Hard herbs, like thyme, sage, and rosemary, can also be used, but it's best to pair them with a tender herb or green so the pesto can blend into the proper consistency. Plus, those herbs tend to have a strong flavor so it's nice to balance them out. The nuts and cheese are flexible, too. Any type of nut, or even seeds like pumpkin, sunflower, or sesame, can be used. For cheese, opt for something hard that's easy to grate. Parmesan is classic, but other Italian cheeses such as Pecorino, aged Asiago, Grana Padano, and ricotta salata are equally great. Or try non-Italian varieties such as Manchego, aged Cheddar, and aged Gouda. I've suggested a few of my favorite equations here, but these are just ideas to get you started. Dig around your pantry to create your own combinations and find your favorites.

—

One quick trick: A chef in Italy taught me to add an ice cube to the food processor. Tossing it in with the herbs shocks them a little and helps prevent the pesto from browning too much.

Place the garlic and nuts into the bowl of a food processor and pulse a few times until roughly chopped.

Add the herbs and ice cube and pulse a few more times until roughly chopped.

Add the olive oil, cheese, lemon juice, and a big pinch of salt. Process, stopping to scrape down the sides of the bowl as needed, until the mixture comes together into a rough paste. Taste and season with more salt, as needed. Use immediately or see storage suggestions following.

To Store

In the fridge: *Pack the pesto into the smallest container in which it can fit—the goal is to limit contact with oxygen so it doesn't brown too much. Pour a thin layer of olive oil over the surface, or press a piece of plastic wrap directly onto surface. Cover and refrigerate for up to 1 week.*

In the freezer: *Even better, thinly spread the pesto onto a wax paper– or parchment paper–lined baking sheet. Press another piece of wax or parchment paper onto the spread pesto and transfer it to the freezer for a few hours to firm up. Once frozen, break up the pesto sheet to fit inside a small zip-top freezer bag and freeze for up to 2 months. When you need it, pull out the bag and break off a bit. Thaw in a bowl on the counter for about 20 minutes or toss it directly into hot pasta, as the heat will quickly defrost it.*

5 Pesto Equations to Try

Walnuts + Basil + Parmesan

Almonds + Parsley (1½ cups, or 42 g) + Thyme (½ cup, or 14 g) + Pecorino

Hazelnuts + Parsley (1½ cups, or 42 g) + Sage (½ cup, or 14 g) + Aged Asiago

Pistachios + Arugula + Ricotta Salata

Almonds + Fennel Fronds + Grana Padano

Freezer Bread Crumbs

1 (1-pound, or 454 g) loaf
country, Italian, or sourdough
bread

—

Makes about 6 cups (about 325 g)

Maybe making your own bread crumbs seems fussy, but let me argue otherwise. You probably already have a whole or partial loaf lying around. If not, a basic loaf costs significantly less than store-bought bread crumbs and will give you enough for months. You also know what's going into your homemade crumbs (just bread, which isn't always the case if you check out the ingredient list on store-bought versions). Keep a bagful in the freezer and your meatballs (see Spaghetti and Meatball Ragu, page 128), chicken (see Baked Chicken Milanese with Lemony Escarole, page 170), and even pasta (see Melted Broccoli Pasta with Capers and Anchovies, page 139) will thank you.

Cut the loaf of bread in half and cut off the crust. Tear half the loaf into roughly 1-inch (2.5 cm) chunks and place them in the bowl of a food processor. Pulse until coarse bread crumbs form, about 40 pulses.

Transfer the crumbs to a large rimmed sheet pan and spread into an even layer. Freeze until firm, about 10 minutes. Transfer the crumbs to a large zip-top freezer bag, seal, and place in the freezer.

Repeat with the remaining half loaf and add those crumbs to the freezer bag. Bread crumbs will keep fresh in the freezer for up to 6 months. Pull out what you need and let defrost a little on the counter for a few minutes before using (no need to thaw completely).

Salsa Verde

½ cup loosely packed (28 g) finely chopped fresh parsley

¼ cup loosely packed (14 g) finely chopped fresh oregano

¼ cup loosely packed (14 g) finely chopped fresh basil

1 garlic clove, grated or minced

1 tablespoon (9 g) capers, finely chopped (rinsed well if salt-packed)

½ cup (120 ml) extra-virgin olive oil

Finely grated zest of ½ lemon

Juice of ½ lemon

1 tablespoon (15 ml) red wine vinegar

Kosher salt

Freshly ground black pepper

Pinch red pepper flakes (optional)

—

Makes about 1 cup (about 230 g)

If you're familiar with chimichurri, consider this the Mediterranean version. In fact, there are countless versions of green sauce—made by combining various herbs with oil and other seasonings—found all over the globe. Pesto is one of them, too, of course. I feel strongly that all green sauces, wherever they've originated, make meals more delicious. This one is garlicky and extra tangy, thanks to both lemon juice and red wine vinegar. I like to add a kick with red pepper flakes, but it doesn't need it to be delicious. Try drizzling this sauce over toast rubbed with tomatoes and topped with creamy burrata (see Tomato Bread with Burrata and Salsa Verde, page 114). It's also a wonderful thing to toss with pasta or cooked grains—or just spoon it over any and all seafood, steak, chicken, vegetables, and eggs.

In a medium bowl, combine the herbs, garlic, and capers. Add the olive oil, lemon zest, lemon juice, vinegar, ¼ teaspoon of salt, several grinds of black pepper, and red pepper flakes (if using). Stir well to combine. Taste and season with more salt and pepper, as needed. Use immediately or refrigerate in an airtight container for up to 1 week. The oil in the salsa verde may cause it to solidify in the cold fridge, so let it warm on the counter for a few minutes and give it a good stir before using.

Everyday Vinaigrette

1 tablespoon (10 g) finely chopped shallot

⅔ cup (160 ml) extra-virgin olive oil

⅓ cup (80 ml) sherry vinegar, or red wine vinegar

1 small garlic clove, grated

2 teaspoons Dijon mustard (regular, whole-grain, or a combination)

Kosher salt

Freshly ground black pepper

—

Makes 1 cup (240 ml)

As a kid, my job in the kitchen was to shake the little packet of Good Seasons Italian Dressing mix with oil and vinegar in the provided glass bottle with the measurements marked right on it. So, I guess you could say I've been a maker of "homemade" dressing from an early age. Years later, I realized it was just as easy to make salad dressing without those packets and it was a whole lot tastier (and better for you, without the extra salt and other additives). I started tinkering with homemade vinaigrette in my first apartment in New York and continued to as my now-husband, Joe, and I moved in together. Soon, he took over and now, after having a simple green salad on the table almost every night, I think we've perfected it.

—

Here's our version. Although the classic oil to vinegar ratio for vinaigrettes is 3 to 1, we prefer a more bracing one so ours is 2 to 1. A good homemade vinaigrette is all about personal taste, though, so after shaking together the ingredients, dip a spoon into it (or better yet, a piece of lettuce), and taste it yourself. If it's too vinegary, add a splash more oil, though do know it will mellow a little when tossed with the salad. This vinaigrette will go with any salad, whether it's a bowl of greens or something with a bit more "stuff" in it.

Rinse the minced shallot well in a fine-mesh strainer with cool water to make it less potent. Drain well and place it in a jar or container with an airtight lid (I usually reach for a Mason jar).

Add the olive oil, vinegar, garlic, Dijon, ½ teaspoon of salt, and several grinds of black pepper. Seal the jar and shake vigorously to emulsify. Taste and add a splash more olive oil and/or a bit more salt and pepper, as needed.

Use immediately or refrigerate for up to 2 weeks. The oil may solidify in the cold fridge, so let the vinaigrette warm on the counter for a few minutes. Shake well before using.

Herb-Infused Honey

1 cup (336 g) mild-flavored honey, such as orange blossom or clover

2 tablespoons (6 g) coarsely chopped fresh herbs, or 1 tablespoon (3 g) dried herbs, such as rosemary, thyme, sage, or lavender

—

Makes 1 cup (336 g)

I am a honey fanatic. Take a look in my pantry and you'll find almost an entire shelf devoted to different types, which I tend to squirrel away and use slowly, to savor each one. Here you want to use a mild-flavored honey, like orange blossom, clover, or wildflower, so the herbs really shine. Hard herbs such as thyme, rosemary, and sage work best here, as they hold up when lightly heated. I also love to use lavender, just be sure to use "food grade" if you're buying it dried. How to use herb-infused honey? Just about anywhere you'd use regular honey. Stir a spoonful into hot tea, dress your morning yogurt, drizzle it on vanilla ice cream, or make a quick cocktail (see Honeyed Prosecco, page 50).

Place the honey and herbs in a small saucepan over low heat and cook until the mixture is warm and fragrant, but not boiling, about 10 minutes. Remove from the heat, cover, and let steep for 10 minutes.

Strain the honey through a fine-mesh strainer into an airtight jar or storage container. Keep refrigerated for up to 1 month. The honey will be cold and a little too thick to drizzle or pour straight from the fridge, so let it warm for a few minutes on the counter before using.

Spicy Chili Oil

1 cup (240 ml) extra-virgin olive oil

1 tablespoon (6 g) red pepper flakes

2 rosemary sprigs (optional)

—

Makes 1 cup (240 ml)

If you're someone who heads right for the bottle of chili oil at your local pizza joint, make this recipe immediately. It's wildly easy to make homemade chili oil and you probably already have the ingredients in your kitchen. Drizzle it over pizza, of course, but also grilled meat, fish, or vegetables—or just use it in place of regular olive oil when roasting vegetables. Try it instead of hot sauce for eggs or better yet, fry or scramble your eggs right in it. You can also swap up to half the amount of regular olive oil for chili oil to make a spicy twist on Everyday Vinaigrette (page 27).

Place the olive oil, red pepper flakes, and rosemary (if using) in a small saucepan over low heat. Cook until the mixture is warm and fragrant, 7 to 10 minutes. Remove from the heat, cover, and let cool to room temperature, about 20 minutes. Transfer the chili oil to an airtight jar or bottle and refrigerate for up to 1 month. It may solidify in the cold fridge, so just bring it to room temperature before using.

Roasted Garlic

1 head garlic, or as many as you like

Extra-virgin olive oil, for drizzling

Kosher salt

—

Makes 1 or more heads roasted garlic

The first time I tasted roasted garlic—when I had cloves scattered all over pizza—I was instantly hooked. I thought it was probably pretty easy to make it myself, so I went home, roasted a whole head, and haven't turned back. If you can turn on an oven, you can make roasted garlic. The cloves become meltingly soft after a stint in the oven and you can squish them right out of their skins. Use roasted garlic as a pizza topping, of course, but also add it to any pasta, make Roasted Garlic–Marinated Olives (page 39) with it, use it in place of raw cloves in Any Herb Pesto (page 20) or Everyday Vinaigrette (page 27), or spread it on crostini for a simple appetizer.

Place a rack in the middle of the oven and preheat the oven to 400°F (200°C).

Peel off the papery outer layers of the garlic head, keeping just a few firm inner layers to keep the head intact.

Cut ¼ to ½ inch (0.6 to 1 cm) crosswise off the top of the garlic head to expose the cloves. Place the garlic, cut-side up, in the middle of a piece of aluminum foil. Drizzle with olive oil, sprinkle with salt, and loosely wrap the garlic in the foil. Roast for about 1 hour until the cloves are deeply golden and caramelized.

Unwrap the garlic and allow it to cool slightly so it's cool enough to handle. Peel away the paper to reveal the roasted cloves or squeeze them out of their paper skins by pressing upward from the bottom of each clove. Use immediately or transfer to an airtight storage container and refrigerate for up to 1 week.

CHAPTER 2

Three-Ingredient (or Fewer) Snacks and Cocktails

Whether I've invited over a few friends for dinner or it's simply a relaxed Saturday night without any guests, having something to snack on and sip while the evening gets going is a must in my book. I, however, under no circumstances, will make it harder on myself than it needs to be. That's where these simple situations come in. Each recipe calls for just two or three ingredients, not including salt, pepper, and olive oil, which are such pantry essentials I consider them passes. They're effortless appetizers and drinks that manage to show off a little when they're the kickoff to a dinner party—or when you're just feeling peckish and thirsty at 5 o'clock on a quiet night in.

Herby Ricotta

2 cups (15 to 16 ounces, or 425 to 454 g, total) high-quality whole milk ricotta

Finely grated zest of 1 lemon

Juice of 1 lemon

½ cup (28 g) loosely packed finely chopped mixed fresh herbs, such as parsley, basil, mint, thyme, rosemary, oregano, tarragon, cilantro, and/or dill

½ teaspoon kosher salt

Freshly ground black pepper

Extra-virgin olive oil, for serving

—

Makes 2 cups (454 g), serving 6 to 8

This is a formula more than a recipe. Stir a bunch of chopped fresh herbs into ricotta, along with some lemon zest and juice and you have something dangerously good. Really, any herbs will do, so gather whatever you have in your garden or your crisper drawer. Serve this ricotta as a dip with crackers or raw vegetables and watch it disappear in no time. Or use it as a condiment: It's great tossed with hot pasta as an impromptu sauce, dolloped on grilled chicken or vegetables, or spread on a thick piece of toast and finished with juicy slices of tomato.

Place the ricotta, lemon zest, lemon juice, herbs, salt, and several grinds of black pepper in a medium bowl. Mix well to combine. Transfer to a serving dish and drizzle with olive oil. Alternatively, refrigerate in an airtight container for up to 3 days and garnish before serving. Serve with crackers or crudités.

Za'atar Pistachios

2 cups (240 g) shelled unsalted raw pistachios

1 tablespoon (15 ml) extra-virgin olive oil

2 tablespoons (14 g) za'atar

½ teaspoon kosher salt

—

Makes 2 cups (254 g), serving 6 to 8

It's easy enough to pick up a bag of seasoned nuts at the grocery store, but making them yourself happens to be just as easy, with even better results. When you're in control, the spices you use and how salty or roasted you want them to be is all up to you. These feel like a real treat, as rich, slightly sweet pistachios aren't something I snack on everyday given their price (though I would if I could!) That said, head to the bulk section of your grocery store or places like Trader Joe's and Costco for the best value. Za'atar (see page 38) makes these pistachios richly aromatic and savory—so, it's wise to have these within reach when you have a glass of wine or a cocktail in hand.

Place a rack in the middle of the oven and preheat the oven to 300°F (150°C).

Spread the pistachios on a rimmed sheet pan. Drizzle with the olive oil and sprinkle with the za'atar and salt. Toss well to coat. Spread into an even layer.

Roast for about 12 minutes, stirring halfway through the cooking time, until toasted and fragrant. Serve warm or at room temperature.

Note:

The nuts will keep well, stored in an air-tight container at room temperature, for up to 3 weeks, so you can make then ahead of time or make a double batch to keep on hand for snacking.

What is Za'atar?

I first discovered za'atar while working at a Lebanese café in college—it's become a spice drawer staple ever since. The Middle Eastern spice blend traditionally starts with a base of dried za'atar, which is the Arabic word for an herb called origanum syriacum, *commonly called Syrian or Lebanese oregano. The herb actually tastes like a combination of thyme, oregano, and marjoram, though. Because it's not easy to source, many blends substitute thyme and oregano for marjoram instead. To this is added toasted sesame seeds, sumac (a spice with a tart, lemon-like flavor), and salt. The blend is incredibly savory and fragrant, and a bit tangy and nutty. It's gained popularity since my college days, so it's fairly easy to find in most spice shops, as well as Middle Eastern grocers. I especially love the blend the artisanal food brand NYShuk makes, which contains the true* origanum syriacum.

7 Ways to Use It

- *Jazz up store-bought pita bread by brushing it with olive oil, sprinkling za'atar on top, and baking until warm.*

- *Add a few generous pinches to whatever vegetables you're roasting when you're tossing them with olive oil, salt, and pepper.*

- *Make that tub of hummus in your fridge more exciting by sprinkling za'atar on top.*

- *Sprinkle it all over chicken or fish before and after baking or grilling.*

- *Stir a spoonful into olive oil to make a dip for bread, or stir it into Greek yogurt to make a dip for vegetable crudités.*

- *Dress up eggs, whether they're scrambled, fried, boiled, or poached, with a dusting.*

- *Roll a log of goat cheese in it for an instant appetizer with crackers or crostini.*

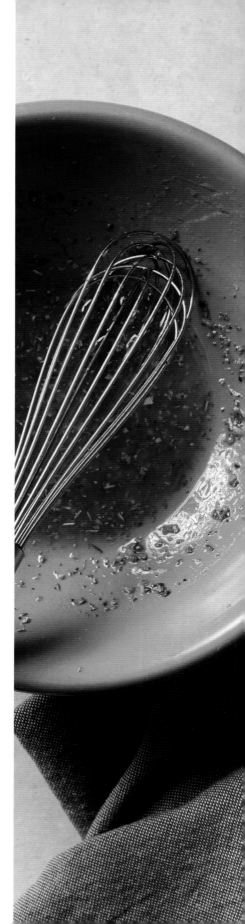

Roasted Garlic–Marinated Olives

2 cups (about 12 ounces, or 340 g) mixed olives, preferably with pits

½ cup (120 ml) extra-virgin olive oil

1 head Roasted Garlic (page 30), cloves removed

1 tablespoon (15 ml) red wine vinegar

—

Makes 2 cups (about 340 g), serving 6 to 8

Once you realize how simple it is to marinate your own olives, you'll forever bypass the overpriced olive bar at your grocery store. It's not only cheaper to do it yourself, there's something pretty impressive about serving your own creation, though no one really needs to know how painless it was. Here, roasted garlic cloves lend their mellow sweetness to whatever type of olives you choose—I like to combine two or three, in a mix of colors and sizes, like Kalamata, Castelvetrano, Gaeta, Cerignola, or Picholine.

In a medium skillet over medium heat, combine the olives, olive oil, roasted garlic cloves, and vinegar. Heat for 5 to 7 minutes, stirring occasionally, until the olives are warmed through and the mixture is fragrant. Transfer to a serving dish and serve warm or at room temperature. Alternatively, transfer to an airtight storage container and refrigerate for up to 2 weeks. Bring to room temperature before serving.

Note:

Although pitted olives save you the hassle of spitting, they lack the depth of flavor unpitted olives deliver and can have a mushy texture due to the brine they soak in absorbing into the inside of the olives. That's why olives with their pits are your best bet here.

Slinky Red Peppers with Capers and Sherry Vinegar

1 (12-ounce, or 340 g) jar roasted red peppers, drained and cut into slices

1 tablespoon (15 ml) extra-virgin olive oil

1 tablespoon (15 ml) sherry vinegar

2 teaspoons capers, chopped if large (rinsed well if salt-packed)

Kosher salt

Freshly ground black pepper

—

Makes 1½ cups (about 220 g), serving 4

Jarred roasted red peppers are a great convenience, but, unfortunately, all that time hanging out in the jar causes them to become pretty muted and bland compared to those made from scratch. Luckily, I've found a way to improve them. Marinate a jar of roasted red peppers with olive oil and sherry vinegar, throw in some capers for a salty, briny bite, and you have something that's much greater than the sum of its parts.

In a medium bowl, combine the roasted peppers, olive oil, vinegar, capers, a pinch of salt, and several grinds of black pepper. Stir and let marinate for about 20 minutes at room temperature, or refrigerate in an airtight container for up to 1 week. Let the peppers come to room temperature before serving with toasted baguette slices or sturdy crackers.

Note:

Although I really like serving this in a bowl alongside toasted baguette slices for DIY crostini, it's also just a nice thing to keep in the refrigerator all week to spoon over meat, fish, or even scrambled eggs.

Cacio e Pepe Farinata

1 cup (120 g) chickpea flour

1 cup (240 ml) water

3 tablespoons (45 ml) olive oil, divided

½ teaspoon kosher salt

Fresh finely grated Pecorino Romano cheese

Freshly ground black pepper

—

Serves 4 to 6

If you travel to Italy's northwestern region of Liguria, you'll find just about every street vendor, bakery, and pizzeria selling farinata. *Travel a bit farther west along the coast into France, and in the region of Provence they'll be selling it, too, but calling it* socca. *No matter what it's called, it's the same delicious thing: a rustic chickpea pancake that's sliced into wedges or squares and eaten as a snack.*

—

The batter is a simple mix of chickpea flour, water, and olive oil that's baked until it blisters, then served warm. Here, it's decidedly not traditional as it takes inspiration from the classic Roman pasta, cacio e pepe, and is showered with Pecorino cheese and black pepper when it's pulled from the oven. Serve it paired with a crisp white or rosé wine, and you'll feel like you've been whisked away to the Riviera via Rome.

In a medium bowl, whisk the chickpea flour, water, 1 tablespoon (15 ml) of olive oil, and salt together until smooth. Cover and let the mixture rest at room temperature for at least 30 minutes, or up to 2 hours, to give the flour time to absorb the water. (The batter can also be refrigerated for up to 12 hours. Transfer it to the counter to take the chill off before baking, while the oven preheats.)

When ready to bake, place a rack in the top third of the oven (6 to 8 inches, or 15 to 20 cm, from the broiling element) and preheat the oven to 450°F (230°C). You want the entire oven to get nice and hot before broiling the farinata so it bakes evenly.

Continues >

Continued

To cook, place a 10-inch (25 cm) cast iron skillet in the oven and turn on the broiler. Let it sit under the broiler for 5 minutes.

Do your best to skim off and discard most of the foam that has formed on the surface of the chickpea flour batter.

Carefully remove the hot skillet from the oven. Add the remaining 2 tablespoons (30 ml) of olive oil and carefully swirl to coat the bottom of the pan. Pour the batter into the skillet and return it to the oven. Broil until the edges of the flatbread are set, the center is firm, and the top is lightly browned in spots, 6 to 10 minutes.

Remove from the oven. Immediately, generously shower the farinata with Pecorino, then top with several generous grinds of black pepper. Let cool for 5 minutes, then carefully slide a flat spatula under the farinata and transfer it to a cutting board. Slice into wedges and serve warm.

Note:

Farinata also happens to be sturdy enough to act as a base for toppings. I love turning it into a meal by piling vegetables on top and calling it a flatbread (see Chickpea Flatbread with Whipped Feta and Marinated Tomatoes, page 90).

Smoky White Bean Hummus

2 (15-ounce, or 425 g) can white beans, drained and rinsed

Juice of 1 lemon

¾ teaspoon smoked paprika, plus more for garnish

1 teaspoon kosher salt

Freshly ground black pepper

½ cup (120 ml) extra-virgin olive oil, plus more for garnish

—

Makes about 2½ cups (about 600 g), serving 8 to 10

Although traditional hummus is made with chickpeas and tahini, it's a dip that definitely lends itself to experimentation. White beans are creamier and have a milder taste than chickpeas, which means they're well suited for bold flavors like smoked paprika. Serve this white bean hummus with pita chips, crackers, or a mix of raw vegetables for dipping.

Place the white beans, lemon juice, smoked paprika, salt, and several grinds of black pepper in the bowl of a food processor. Blend until smooth, stopping to scrape down the sides of the bowl as needed, 25 to 30 seconds.

With the food processor running, drizzle in the olive oil and continue to blend until very smooth and creamy, 1 to 2 minutes more. Transfer to a serving dish and garnish with a drizzle of olive oil and sprinkle of paprika. Alternatively, store in an airtight container in the refrigerator for up to 1 week and garnish before serving.

Fennel and Parmesan "Crostini"

1 medium fennel bulb

Freshly shaved Parmesan cheese

Extra-virgin olive oil

Freshly ground black pepper

—

Makes about 16

I tend to lean toward bites that get you hungry for dinner rather than fill you up before sitting down to eat. This light recipe is just that. Take crunchy fennel slices, top them with salty shaved Parmesan and a bit of good olive oil, and you have a 5-minute appetizer that's gets your stomach excited for the main attraction.

Cut off the stalks from the fennel bulb and reserve a handful of fronds for garnish. Trim off about ¼ inch (0.6 cm) from the browned root end of the fennel bulb. Halve the bulb vertically. If the outer layers of either bulb half are browned or dried out, peel them away, then slice each bulb half through the root, to keep the layers held together, into ¼-inch (0.6 cm)-thick wedges. You should end up with about 16 thin wedges. If any pieces fall off in the process, save them, too, for snacking or to toss into a salad.

Lay the fennel wedges on a serving plate. Top each with a couple shavings of Parmesan cheese. Drizzle with olive oil. Coarsely chop the reserved fronds and sprinkle over the top. Garnish with several grinds of black pepper and serve.

Note:

If your fennel bulb has lots of fronds attached, save what you don't use for garnish to make Any Herb Pesto (page 20)! Don't worry about having to make a batch right away, though: The fronds will stay fresh, stored loosely in a plastic bag in your vegetable crisper drawer, for a couple of days.

Fig in a Pig

10 fresh figs, or dried figs

4 ounces (113 g) soft, spreadable cheese, such as goat cheese or blue cheese

10 thin prosciutto slices, halved lengthwise

—

Makes 20

This playful snack is one of the many ways I celebrate fresh figs when they come around in late summer. Because their season is so short, however, and the combination of sweet fruit with salty prosciutto and creamy cheese is always such a crowd-pleaser, I've learned to adapt the recipe for the months when I can't get fresh figs. These can be made 365 days a year by substituting dried figs. The cheese is flexible, too: anything creamy and spreadable, from goat or blue cheese to Brie or Camembert, works. Don't hesitate to experiment to find your favorite match. And, if you're game to break the rules and add a fourth ingredient, you just may want to finish these with a drizzle of honey.

Place a rack in the middle of the oven and preheat the oven to 425°F (220°C). Line a baking sheet with parchment paper.

If using dried figs and they are especially dry, place them in a small bowl, bring some water to a boil, then pour it over the figs to cover them. Let sit for 5 to 10 minutes, then drain the figs, discarding the liquid, and lightly pat them dry. Otherwise, if the dried figs are already quite plump, there's no need to soak them.

Halve the figs through the stem. Spread about ½ teaspoon of cheese on the cut side of the fig halves. Wrap a strip of prosciutto around each fig half, overlapping it so it sticks to itself. Place the figs, cut-side up, on the prepared baking sheet.

Roast until the prosciutto browns and crisps, 10 to 12 minutes. Serve warm.

Honeyed Prosecco

1 ounce (30 ml) fresh lemon juice

½ ounce (15 ml) water

½ ounce (14 g) Herb-Infused Honey (page 28), or regular honey

About 6 ounces (180 ml) chilled prosecco

—

Serves 1

This is a cocktail that lends itself well to gatherings. Multiply the honey, water, and lemon juice depending on how many you plan to serve. Combine the three ahead of time and, when needed, shake with ice, divide among glasses, and top off each glass with prosecco. It's a drink that feels a little fancy yet is wildly fast to prepare.

Place the lemon juice, water, and honey in a cocktail shaker and stir to dissolve the honey. Add ice. Cover and shake vigorously until well chilled, about 15 seconds. Strain into a Champagne flute or coupe and top off with chilled prosecco.

Americano

1½ ounces (45 ml) Cappelletti Aperitivo, or Campari

1½ ounces (45 ml) sweet vermouth

Club soda, for topping off

Orange slice or twist, for garnish (optional)

—

Serves 1

If it's Friday night, you'll most likely find my husband, Joe, and me at home sipping Americanos. The not-too-strong cocktail is our favorite way to ease into the weekend. Although the bitter apéritif Campari is traditional here, I highly recommend seeking out Cappelletti Aperitivo. It's a little less bitter, which means it's much more approachable. I also like that it's made without any artificial coloring.

In a rocks glass filled with ice, combine the Cappelletti and sweet vermouth. Top off with club soda and garnish with an orange slice or twist, if desired.

Get to Know Cappelletti Aperitivo

Although Aperol and Campari have become pervasive in bars and restaurants thanks to the popularity of cocktails such as the Aperol Spritz and Negroni, Cappelletti Aperitivo is a bit like the middle child of the family. All three are Italian liqueurs that are vibrantly red or orange hued and bitter, thanks to their own unique mix of botanicals, and enjoyed as an apéritif or in Italian, an aperitivo. Cappelletti tends to go quietly unnoticed, which is a shame because it's arguably the best.

Whereas Aperol can skew too sweet and Campari's bracing bitterness is an acquired taste, Cappelletti falls perfectly in between. It's more approachable than Campari and drier and more balanced than Aperol.

Unlike its siblings who are made from a neutral spirit, Cappelletti's base is wine, which gives it a rounder, gentler flavor that allows the botanicals to shine a bit more. It also happens to get its ruby red color from natural sources rather than artificial ones (Campari used to as well but made the switch in 2006). So it's well worth making space for a bottle on your bar cart. (See the top right photo on page 17 for a visual reference of what to search for in stores.)

Limonata Smash

4 fresh mint leaves, plus an extra sprig for garnish

2 ounces (60 ml) bourbon

5 to 6 ounces (150 to 180 ml) San Pellegrino Limonata

—

Serves 1

If you're never had Limonata, this cocktail is the perfect excuse to pick some up. The Italian lemon soda used to be hard to find outside Italy, but it's now available at most major grocery stores and, of course, online. There are also a handful of other fun flavors—like blood orange and grapefruit—that are equally as cocktail worthy, so feel free to experiment!

Muddle the mint leaves in a rocks glass. Add the bourbon and some ice cubes. Top off with Limonata.

How to Muddle

If you've sipped a Mojito, you've had a drink that's been muddled. This technique is called for in a number of cocktail recipes, but if you don't make many drinks at home, you may be scratching your head as to how to do it. Muddling is simply the act of crushing fresh ingredients, like herbs, fruit, or even cucumber slices, to draw out their flavors so they easily mix with and flavor the alcohol. A specific tool, aptly called a muddler, is used to do this, though if you don't have one, you can use a pestle from a mortar and pestle or the end of a wooden spoon.

To muddle, place the ingredient, such as the mint leaves in the Limonata Smash, in the bottom of a sturdy glass, press down lightly, and twist. Pounding might seem faster but you'll end up with bitter herbs or overly bruised fruit. With a light hand, once you smell the herbs, or the fruit is crushed and released its juices, you're good to go.

Cocchi Americano Spritz

3 ounces (90 ml) Cocchi
Americano Bianco

3 to 6 ounces (90 to 180 ml)
tonic water

Lemon slice or twist, for garnish
(optional)

—

Serves 1

I prefer my cocktails to be light and easy, so they don't knock me over before it's even time for dinner. That's why I am a huge fan of the Italian apéritif wine called Cocchi Americano Bianco. It's less boozy than hard alcohol and off-dry, with just a touch of bitterness. It can be turned into all sorts of fancy cocktails but it really doesn't need much more than a generous splash of tonic water.

Fill a highball or Collins glass with ice and pour in the Cocchi Americano. Top off with tonic water. Garnish with a lemon slice or twist, if desired.

What Exactly is Cocchi Americano Bianco?

Cocchi Americano Bianco is a white apéritif wine that's aromatized with botanicals such as cinchona (the bitter bark that makes quinine), citrus peel, and elderflower. It's light and crisp with a sweetness that's balanced by a delicately bitter edge.

The traditional formula is made with white wine, though over the years, they've developed a red wine–based version called Cocchi Americano Rosa. Although similar to the original, it has berry notes from the red wine base and contains a slightly different variation of botanicals, such as rose petals and saffron, which lends floral aromas. It also works great in this cocktail.

Both versions are relatively low in alcohol as compared to spirits, just 16.5 percent ABV, so they're especially nice to sip before dinner. Oh, and a bottle won't set you back more than $20. Once open, store it in the fridge and enjoy it within a month or two—though it's dangerously easy to get through a bottle much sooner.

CHAPTER 3

Salads and Soups

I grew up with a salad on the dinner table every night, and it's a habit I can't shake. I find it's just about the easiest way to squeeze an extra serving of vegetables onto my plate, and I've always appreciated the crunchy, cold contrast it lends to whatever else is part of the meal. Often, however, the salad *is* the meal when I've loaded it with a bunch of extra-satisfying things.

Though, if it were up to my husband, Joe, the meal would be soup. I've never met someone so passionate about bowls of broth, and, honestly, I wouldn't be surprised if he had soup running through his veins. I tease him about it but the truth is I love how easy it is to toss lots of wholesome things into a simmering pot and transform them into something so much greater than the sum of their parts, so I never complain about the fact that soup is just as much of a staple on our dinner table.

Asparagus Salad with Radishes, Snap Peas, and Avocado

Kosher salt

8 ounces (227 g) sugar snap peas, tough strings removed

2 tablespoons (30 ml) extra-virgin olive oil

Juice of 1 lemon

1 teaspoon Dijon mustard

Freshly ground black pepper

12 ounces (340 g) thick asparagus, woody ends trimmed

1 small bunch radishes (5 or 6), tops removed, thinly sliced

3 scallions, white and green parts, thinly sliced

1 avocado, pitted, peeled, and cut into 1-inch (2.5 cm) chunks

Flaky sea salt (optional)

—

Serves 4 to 6

After a long winter of eating nothing but root vegetables, there's nothing quite like seeing the first bunches of bright green asparagus hit the farmers' market in early spring. For the short few weeks it's in season, I'll happily gorge on asparagus for breakfast, lunch, and dinner. This salad is one of my favorites. It celebrates the freshest asparagus by forgoing cooking it altogether. Instead, the stalks are shaved into thin ribbons and joined with two other spring favorites, crisp snap peas and pretty pink radishes. It's the perfect dinner companion to any meat or fish, particularly on those first balmy evenings of the season when you decide to grill, but it's also a salad that could easily pass for a not-too-heavy lunch, thanks to plenty of buttery avocado chunks. Slide a fried or poached egg onto each serving if you're a little hungrier, or if you'd rather call it brunch.

Fill a large bowl with ice and water and set aside.

Bring a medium pot of salted water to a boil over high heat. Add the snap peas and cook until they are vibrant green and tender but still crisp, about 1 minute. Drain and immediately transfer the peas to the ice water.

In a large bowl, whisk the olive oil, lemon juice, Dijon, a generous pinch of salt, and several grinds of black pepper until combined and emulsified.

Working one asparagus spear at a time, hold onto the tip and use a vegetable peeler to shave the asparagus stalk lengthwise into thin strips. Add the shaved asparagus to the bowl of vinaigrette as you go. You'll likely be left with a bit of each spear that's too difficult to peel. Use a sharp knife to slice these pieces thinly, as best you can, and add them to the bowl. Add any tips that may have snapped off in the process to the bowl as well.

Drain the snap peas and thinly slice them lengthwise. Add the snap peas, along with any small inner green peas that fell out when slicing, the radishes, and scallions to the bowl and toss to evenly coat in the dressing.

Add the avocado and gently toss to combine. Taste and season with additional salt and pepper, as needed. Garnish with a few pinches of flaky sea salt, if desired, and serve.

Mixed Melon and Prosciutto Caprese

3 to 3½ pounds (1.4 to 1.6 kg) melon, such as cantaloupe, honeydew, and/or watermelon, peeled, quartered, and thinly sliced widthwise into crescent moon pieces

8 ounces (227 g) fresh mozzarella, sliced into rounds

2 ounces (55 g) thinly sliced prosciutto

Extra-virgin olive oil

Flaky sea salt

Freshly ground black pepper

Handful fresh basil leaves

—

Serves 4 to 6

In summertime, cantaloupe and prosciutto is a classic Italian combination. It makes sense, as the sweet, juicy melon pairs so perfectly with the salty ham. Other melons, such as honeydew and watermelon, are less traditional but equally a great match. Here, creamy mozzarella and peppery basil join the party in a fresh and colorful twist on a caprese salad.

—

For wow factor, I like to use a mix of all three melons, but opting for just one or two will achieve winning results, too (and won't leave you with lots of leftover melon halves in the fridge). It's totally your call.

Arrange the melon and mozzarella slices in an overlapping pattern on a platter. Tear the prosciutto and arrange the pieces over the top. Drizzle with olive oil and sprinkle with a few pinches of flaky sea salt and several grinds of black pepper. Tear the basil leaves into small pieces, if large, otherwise keep them whole. Scatter the basil over the top and serve.

Mediterranean Niçoise Salad

This composed French salad has everything going for it: there's minimal cooking involved, it's full of feel-good ingredients, it has enough substance to keep you satisfied, and perhaps, most importantly, it pairs perfectly with cold rosé. This twist takes the best elements of the salad—good tuna, sweet tomatoes, crisp green beans, tender potatoes—and combines them with a few extra Mediterranean favorites, like marinated artichokes and lots of fresh basil. Anchovies are classic in Niçoise, but here they're featured in the vinaigrette rather than added whole, so their umami flavor is evenly distributed. The vinaigrette is also bolstered with briny capers and earthy oregano to add more Mediterranean flair.

For Vinaigrette:

¼ cup (60 ml) extra-virgin olive oil

Juice of 1 lemon

2 teaspoons Dijon mustard

2 teaspoon capers, chopped (rinsed well if salt-packed)

2 oil-packed anchovy fillets, finely chopped

1 garlic clove, grated or minced

1 teaspoon finely chopped fresh oregano

Freshly ground black pepper

For Salad:

4 large eggs

8 ounces (227 g) small red-skinned potatoes

Kosher salt

4 ounces (113 g) green beans, stemmed

4 ounces (about 4 packed cups; 113 g) arugula

1 cup (150 g) cherry tomatoes, or grape tomatoes, halved

2 (5-ounce, or 140 g) cans oil-packed tuna, drained

1 (12-ounce, or 340 g) jar marinated and quartered artichoke hearts, drained

½ cup (78 g) Niçoise, Taggiasca, or Kalamata olives, pitted

Coarsely chopped fresh basil leaves, for serving

Freshly ground black pepper

Flaky sea salt (optional)

To make the vinaigrette: In a small bowl, whisk the olive oil, lemon juice, Dijon, capers, anchovies, garlic, oregano, and a few grinds of black pepper until combined and emulsified. Set aside.

To make the salad: Let the eggs rest on the counter to take their chill off from the fridge while you cook the potatoes—this will help prevent them from cracking when boiled.

Place the potatoes in a medium pot and cover with a few inches (about 7.5 cm) of cold water. Bring the water to a boil. Add a few generous pinches of salt and cook the potatoes until fork-tender, 10 to 15 minutes. Using a slotted spoon, remove the potatoes and set aside to cool.

Continues >

Serves 4

Continued

Return the pot of water to a boil. Using a slotted spoon, carefully lower the eggs into the water. Boil, uncovered, for 7 minutes for softboiled eggs with jammy, but not runny, yolks, or 10 minutes for hardboiled eggs with firm but still creamy yolks.

Meanwhile, fill a medium bowl with ice and water.

Using a slotted spoon, transfer the eggs to the ice bath. Chill until cold, about 5 minutes, then remove, peel, halve lengthwise, and set aside.

Return the pot of water to a boil once more and add the green beans. Cook until they are vibrant green and tender but still crisp, about 2 minutes. Using a slotted spoon, transfer the green beans to the ice bath. Chill until cold, about 1 minute. Remove, pat dry, and set aside.

Halve the potatoes, place them in a large bowl, and toss with ½ tablespoon of vinaigrette.

Spread the arugula on a large platter, or divide it among 4 individual plates or shallow bowls. Whisk the vinaigrette once or twice more to ensure it's emulsified and drizzle a bit over the arugula. Arrange the potatoes on one section of your platter or divide among the plates.

Repeat the tossing process with the green beans and tomatoes, tossing each separately with ½ tablespoon of vinaigrette and arranging them in sections on your platter or plates.

Arrange the eggs, tuna, and artichokes in the remaining sections of the platter or plates. Scatter olives over the top and drizzle with the remaining vinaigrette. Sprinkle with basil, a few grinds of black pepper, and a few pinches of flaky sea salt, if desired, and serve.

About Those Olives

Taggiasca olives are the Italian equivalent to Niçoise olives—they're produced in Liguria, the region of Italy that borders the area of France where Niçoise olives are grown, and are fun to try here. Both Taggiasca and Niçoise olives are petite, sweet, and mild—but aren't always easy to find. Luckily, Kalamata olives, though larger and richer in flavor, will do the job if you can't find either of the others.

Peak-Summer Panzanella

Once the sweetest, juiciest tomatoes start coming around in late July and into August, I pretty much subsist on this panzanella. I declare impromptu picnics so we can bring it to the park for lunch, pick up some prosciutto and cheese to serve next to it for a weekly no-cook dinner, and carry it along to just about every potluck and cookout. My version of the Tuscan bread salad doesn't veer too far from tradition; though cucumbers don't always make an appearance, I just love their crunch against the soggy chunks of bread and soft tomatoes. Just to be sure, soggy is a good thing here: It means the bread soaked up so much of the garlicky vinaigrette and bowl juices that it's practically bloated.

1 small shallot, halved lengthwise and thinly sliced

½ loaf (6 to 8 ounces, or 170 to 227 g) good sourdough bread, or country-style bread

5 tablespoons (75 ml) extra-virgin olive oil, divided

Kosher salt

Freshly ground black pepper

3 tablespoons (45 ml) red wine vinegar

1 tablespoon (9 g) capers, chopped if large (rinsed well if salt-packed)

1 teaspoon Dijon mustard

1 small garlic clove, grated or minced

2 pounds (908 g) heirloom tomatoes, or beefsteak tomatoes, cut into 1-inch (2.5 cm) chunks

½ large English cucumber, halved lengthwise and cut into slices

½ cup (20 g) loosely packed chopped mixed fresh herbs, such as parsley, basil, thyme, oregano, and/or mint

Flaky sea salt (optional)

—

Serves 4 to 6

Place a rack in the top third of the oven and preheat the oven to 425°F (220°C).

Place the sliced shallot in a small bowl and pour in enough water to cover by about ½ inch (1 cm). Set aside to make the shallot less potent while you toast the bread and make the vinaigrette.

Slice or tear the bread into roughly 1-inch (2.5 cm) cubes (you should have about 4 cups) and place on a rimmed sheet pan. Drizzle with 2 tablespoons (30 ml) of olive oil, season with salt and pepper, toss to coat, and spread into an even layer. Bake, tossing halfway through, until dry and pale golden brown, 6 to 8 minutes.

Meanwhile, in a large bowl, whisk the remaining 3 tablespoons (45 ml) of olive oil, the vinegar, capers, Dijon, garlic, a big pinch of salt, and several grinds of black pepper until combined and emulsified.

Continues >

Continued

Drain the shallot slices and pat dry. Add them to the vinaigrette along with the tomatoes and cucumber and toss to coat.

Once the bread cubes are toasted, let cool for 5 minutes, then add them to the bowl and toss well to combine and coat in the vinaigrette and tomato juices. Add the herbs and toss again.

Let rest at room temperature for at least 30 minutes and up to 4 hours, tossing occasionally, to distribute evenly the juices and vinaigrette. Taste and season with additional salt and pepper, as needed. Toss again and sprinkle with a pinch of flaky sea salt, if desired, before serving.

Note:

This is a perfect make-ahead salad as it actually improves after a nice long rest—the bread will soak up more goodness and all the flavors will have more time to mingle. And because it doesn't need to be refrigerated while it's doing its thing, you can easily transport it to your picnic or party. I will say, though, after 4 hours, the bread will start to get a little too soggy and begin to fall apart, so do dig into the panzanella before that happens.

Hot Smoked Salmon Greek Salad

½ small red onion, thinly sliced

¾ cup (170 g) whole milk plain Greek yogurt, divided

2 tablespoons (30 ml) extra-virgin olive oil

2 tablespoons (30 ml) red wine vinegar

1 tablespoon (15 ml) fresh lemon juice

1 garlic clove, grated or minced

¾ teaspoon dried oregano, plus more for finishing

Kosher salt

Freshly ground black pepper

2 heads (about 1 pound, or 454 g, total) butter lettuce, such as Boston or Bibb, torn into bite-size pieces

1 pint (about 2 cups, or 300 g), cherry tomatoes, or grape tomatoes, halved

½ large English cucumber, quartered lengthwise and cut into slices

½ cup (78 g) Kalamata olives, pitted and halved lengthwise

2 (4-ounce, or 115 g) hot smoked salmon fillets

—

Serves 4

When you think of smoked salmon, the cold stuff that's sliced paper thin and piled on top of a bagel is probably what first comes to mind. I am a big fan of cold smoked salmon (and the bagel, too, of course), but hot smoked salmon gives it some major competition. It's often forgotten about and really shouldn't be because it's easily more of a crowd-pleaser. It wins over those who aren't fans of the cold rawness of the other stuff because, well, it's actually cooked. It's got all the nice flakiness of regular cooked salmon with the added benefit of rich, smoky flavor.

—

What's more? All the cooking is done for you, so you simply have to buy it and flake it onto whatever you so choose. In warmer weather, when no-cook meals are essential to keep the kitchen cool, I stock a piece of hot smoked salmon in the fridge at all times, ready to turn regular salads into dinner salads. Here it adds flair to the classic Greek salad. And although some may say this salad isn't truly Greek without feta, both the smoked salmon and olives provide plenty of salty bite. Instead, I find piling the salad onto plates of creamy Greek yogurt better suited here. The yogurt provides welcomed tang every time you swipe up a forkful of salad from your plate.

Place the sliced red onion in a small bowl and pour in enough water to cover by about ½ inch (1 cm). Set aside for about 10 minutes to make the onion less potent.

Meanwhile, divide the yogurt among 4 shallow bowls or plates. Use the back of a spoon to spread it evenly over the bottom of the dishes.

In a large bowl, whisk the olive oil, vinegar, lemon juice, garlic, oregano, a generous pinch of salt, and a few grinds of black pepper until combined and emulsified.

Drain the onion slices and pat dry. Add them to the vinaigrette along with the lettuce, tomatoes, cucumber, and olives. Toss to coat. Taste and season with additional salt and pepper, as needed.

Divide the salad among the prepared bowls, piling it on top of the yogurt. Flake the salmon into large chunks with your hands or a fork and place some on top of each salad. Sprinkle each salad with a pinch of oregano, and serve.

Note:

I really love the salty flavor and semi-firm texture of ricotta salata, but an equal amount of feta is a nice replacement. Or try goat cheese if you crave something creamy or blue cheese if you want to add a little funk.

Warm Roasted Delicata Squash and Kale Salad

For Vinaigrette:

3 tablespoons (45 ml) extra-virgin olive oil

2 tablespoons (30 ml) sherry vinegar

1 teaspoon Dijon mustard

1 small garlic clove, grated or minced

Kosher salt

Freshly ground black pepper

For Salad:

1 large (about 1 pound, or 454 g, total) delicata squash, halved lengthwise, seeded, and cut into ½-inch (1 cm) slices

1 medium red onion, halved lengthwise and cut into 1-inch (2.5 cm) wedges

2 tablespoons (30 ml) olive oil

Kosher salt

Freshly ground black pepper

2 medium or 1 large bunch (about 12 ounces, or 340 g, total) lacinato kale, stems removed and leaves torn into bite-size pieces

4 ounces (113 g) ricotta salata cheese, crumbled (about 1 cup)

½ cup (70 g) hazelnuts, toasted and roughly chopped

—

Serves 4 to 6

Even though I consider myself fairly capable when it comes to wielding a knife in the kitchen, I always hold my breath when attempting to cut through winter squashes such as butternut and acorn. I have yet to lose a finger, but, honestly, it's only a matter of time, which is why delicata squash has won my affection. Not only is it a hundred times easier to cut, it doesn't need to be peeled. Here, half-moons of delicata squash are roasted alongside chucks of red onion until soft and caramelized, then tossed, while still warm, with tender kale, toasty hazelnuts, and salty ricotta salata cheese in a sweet and savory sherry vinaigrette. It's a salad I could very well eat weekly through the fall and winter without tiring of it (which I say with confidence because I've definitely done it).

Place a rack in the middle of the oven and preheat the oven to 425°F (220°C).

To make the vinaigrette: In a small bowl, whisk the olive oil, vinegar, Dijon, garlic, a generous pinch of salt, and a few grinds of black pepper until combined and emulsified.

To make the salad: Place the squash and red onion on a rimmed sheet pan. Drizzle with the olive oil, season with salt and black pepper, and toss to coat. Spread the vegetables into an even layer. Roast, carefully flipping halfway through, until tender and lightly caramelized, 20 to 25 minutes.

Place the kale in a large bowl. Using your hands, massage the leaves for about 1 minute or so until they feel less stiff. Whisk the vinaigrette once or twice more to ensure it's emulsified, then drizzle about half of it over the kale and toss to coat.

Once the vegetables are roasted, add them to the bowl with the kale. Drizzle in the remaining vinaigrette and toss gently to combine, being careful not to break up the tender squash. Add the ricotta salata and hazelnuts. Toss gently once more. Taste and season with additional salt and pepper, as needed. Serve warm or at room temperature.

The Easiest Arugula Salad

2 tablespoons (30 ml) extra-virgin olive oil

Juice of 1 lemon

Kosher salt

Freshly ground black pepper

5 ounces (about 5 packed cups; 142 g) arugula

Freshly shaved Parmesan cheese, or ½ large fennel bulb, shaved on a mandoline or thinly sliced (optional)

—

Serves 4 to 6

I don't use the term "easiest" lightly, but truly, this is the salad I make almost every single night because it really is that simple. It also pairs with just about anything you're serving for dinner, whether it's a colorful pasta (page 117), Thyme Pesto Roast Chicken with Crispy Potatoes (page 148), or even just take-out pizza. It's a light side that gives you your dinner dose of greens.

—

Prepare this salad as you like it, depending on your taste or what you happen to have in the fridge. You can serve it plainly, with just arugula, or add an extra component. I love the fresh, crunchy bite fennel delivers but if you're not a fan, shaved Parmesan cheese is a great substitute (and always a crowd-pleaser).

In a large bowl, whisk the olive oil, lemon juice, a generous pinch of salt, and several grinds of black pepper until combined and emulsified. Add the arugula and toss to combine. Add some shaved Parmesan or the fennel, if desired, and toss once or twice more to combine. Taste and season with additional salt and pepper, as needed, and serve.

Roasted Greek Tomato Soup

2 (28-ounce, or 794 g) cans whole peeled tomatoes

3 garlic cloves, smashed and peeled

4 tablespoons (60 ml) extra-virgin olive oil, divided, plus more for garnish

Kosher salt

Freshly ground black pepper

1 medium yellow onion, finely chopped

¼ cup (65 g) tomato paste

1 teaspoon dried oregano

½ teaspoon ground cinnamon

¼ teaspoon red pepper flakes

4 cups (1 L) low-sodium vegetable broth, or chicken broth

Coarsely chopped fresh parsley, for serving

—

Serves 6

Note:

Why roast canned tomatoes? It helps concentrate their flavor, which lends extra depth and richness to the soup. Don't expect them to brown and caramelize like roasted vegetables, though. They're so juicy straight from the can they'll never really take on that color. Instead, their red hue will deepen and they'll become meltingly soft and jammy. That's exactly what you want.

When you think about which herbs and spices pair well with tomatoes, cinnamon is probably not the first one that comes to mind. Basil, sure, but the sweet spice you sprinkle on your oatmeal? Well, actually, yes. Ground cinnamon is a common addition to tomato dishes in Greek cuisine and the pair is one worth getting to know. The spice brings out the natural sweetness of tomatoes while balancing their acidity and lending a touch of earthy, grounding flavor. You don't need much for it to be effective. Rather than this tomato soup tasting boldly of cinnamon, the spice sings quietly in the background. Those who don't know it's there may not realize it at first, with garlic and red pepper flakes taking the lead, but will wonder what is making their spoonfuls different than the usual.

Place a rack in the middle of the oven and preheat the oven to 425°F (220°C).

Remove the whole tomatoes from the cans with a fork, reserving the liquid, and place them in a 9 × 13-inch (23 × 33 cm) or other 3-quart (3 L) baking dish. Using the fork, gently press down on the tomatoes to flatten them slightly. Scatter the garlic over the tomatoes and drizzle with 2 tablespoons (30 ml) of olive oil. Season with ½ teaspoon of salt and several grinds of black pepper. Roast, stirring halfway through, until the tomatoes are soft and jammy, and some, but not all, of the liquid in the baking dish has reduced, 40 to 45 minutes.

Meanwhile, heat the remaining 2 tablespoons (30 ml) of olive oil in a large Dutch oven over medium heat. Add the onion and sauté until softened and translucent, 3 to 5 minutes. Add the tomato paste, oregano, cinnamon, and red pepper flakes. Sauté until the paste has deepened in color, about 1 minute. Remove from the heat.

When the tomato and garlic mixture is ready, carefully transfer it to the pot. Add the reserved tomato liquid from the cans, the broth, and ½ teaspoon of salt. Stir to combine and return the pot to the heat, bringing the soup to a boil. Reduce the heat to maintain a gentle simmer, cover the pot with the lid ajar, and simmer for about 20 minutes to allow the flavors to meld.

Working in batches, transfer the soup to a stand blender and purée until smooth. Or, use an immersion blender right in the pot to blend the soup until smooth. Taste and season with additional salt and pepper, as needed. Serve garnished with parsley and a drizzle of olive oil.

Cucumber Tahini Gazpacho with Crispy Spiced Chickpeas

When it's mid-summer and too hot to even think about cooking, make this soup. Toss a handful of things in a blender and, before you know it, you have something cool and refreshing yet surprisingly satisfying. The latter is thanks to tahini, the sesame seed paste that's most commonly used to make hummus. It lends creaminess and nutty flavor but, more importantly, it adds a bit of protein and healthy fat, which turns this chilled soup into a light meal. My favorite part, though, is the crispy spiced chickpeas. They also add protein but, really, they're there for the textural contrast they give every spoonful. Just be sure to make them right before you serve the soup, as they'll lose their crunch if made too far in advance.

For Gazpacho

½ cup (115 g) tahini, well stirred

½ cup (120 ml) water

¼ cup (60 ml) extra-virgin olive oil, plus more for garnish

Juice of 1 lemon

1 cup (28 g) packed fresh basil leaves

1 cup (28 g) packed fresh cilantro, plus more for garnish

2 large (about 2 pounds, or 908 g, total) English cucumbers, unpeeled and roughly chopped

1 small shallot, roughly chopped

1 garlic clove, roughly chopped

Kosher salt

Freshly ground black pepper

For Crispy Spiced Chickpeas:

1 (15-ounce, or 425 g) can chickpeas, drained, rinsed, and patted dry

2 teaspoons extra-virgin olive oil

1 teaspoon ground cumin

¼ teaspoon kosher salt

—

Serves 4 to 6

To make the gazpacho: Place all the ingredients, along with 1 teaspoon of kosher salt and several grinds of black pepper, in a blender, preferably high-speed. Blend until completely smooth, stopping to scrape down the sides of the blender, as needed. Taste and season with additional salt and pepper, as needed.

Transfer the gazpacho to the refrigerator to chill for at least 1 hour and up to 1 day. Taste again and season with additional salt and pepper, as needed, before serving.

To make the crispy spiced chickpeas: (Make these right before serving as they'll lose their crunch if made too far in advance.)

Place a rack in the middle of the oven and preheat the oven to 450°F (230°C).

Place the chickpeas on a rimmed sheet pan. Drizzle with olive oil, sprinkled with cumin and salt, and toss well to coat. Spread into an even layer. Roast, tossing halfway through, until crispy and lightly browned in spots, 18 to 20 minutes. Let cool for 5 to 10 minutes.

To serve, divide the gazpacho among bowls and top with the crispy chickpeas. Garnish with a few cilantro leaves and a drizzle of olive oil.

Spicy Sausage and Rice Soup

1 tablespoon (15 ml) extra-virgin olive oil

1 pound (454 g) hot Italian sausage, or sweet Italian sausage (chicken, turkey, or pork), casings removed if using links

1 medium yellow onion, finely chopped

Kosher salt

Freshly ground black pepper

2 garlic cloves, minced

4 cups (960 ml) low-sodium chicken broth

1 (15-ounce, or 425 g) can diced tomatoes

½ cup (95 g) long-grain brown rice, rinsed well

¼ cup (10 g) loosely packed chopped fresh basil leaves

Freshly shaved Parmesan cheese, for serving

—

Serves 4 to 6

I am not going to lie and say the pizza place we would order take-out from growing up was a super-authentic hole-in-the-wall because it definitely wasn't: It was a place called Bertucci's, which is a wide-spread Italian chain in Massachusetts and throughout the Northeast. What I remember about it, though, wasn't the pizza—it was the soup. Every time we called in an order, my mom would order a cup of their Italian sausage soup. I was usually too busy scarfing down my slices to pay much attention, but when I finally did try a spoonful from her cup, I became hooked just like her. This is my home-made take on that childhood favorite.

—

Go ahead and use whatever type of Italian sausage you like—chicken or pork, hot or sweet. Don't veer from the brown rice, however. Not only because of its whole-grain goodness, but also because brown rice actually holds up better in the soup and won't turn to mush when you reheat leftover bowls.

Heat the olive oil in a large Dutch oven over medium-high heat. Add the sausage and cook, breaking it up with a wooden spoon, until browned and cooked through, 5 to 7 minutes.

Add the onion, season with salt and pepper, and sauté until softened and translucent, 3 to 5 minutes. Add the garlic and sauté until fragrant, about 1 minute. Pour in the chicken broth along with the tomatoes and their juices. Bring to a boil, then lower the heat to a simmer.

Stir in the rice and continue to simmer gently, covered but with the lid slightly ajar, stirring occasionally, until the rice is tender, 35 to 40 minutes.

Taste and season with additional salt and pepper, as needed. Stir in the basil and serve garnished with shaved Parmesan.

Garlic Parmesan Soup with Greens and Beans

For Broth:

2 heads garlic

2 tablespoons (30 ml) extra-virgin olive oil

8 cups (2 L) water

2 large Parmesan cheese rinds

2 sage sprigs

Kosher salt

Freshly ground black pepper

Red pepper flakes (optional)

For Soup:

2 (15-ounce, or 425 g) cans white beans, such as cannellini, drained and rinsed

1 bunch (about 8 ounces, or 227 g) hearty greens, such as kale, Swiss chard, or mustard greens, stemmed, leaves torn into bite-size pieces

Finely grated zest of ½ lemon

Juice of ½ lemon

Freshly shaved Parmesan cheese, for serving

—

Serves 4 to 6

I don't always have chicken or vegetable broth on hand when a soup craving strikes, which is why I've always been drawn to recipes that start with plain old water, like this one. Consider this a quick, pantry-style broth: Bolster a pot of water with simple ingredients, like garlic, Parmesan, and herbs, and you've got a light yet flavorful base for something cozy. The trick is to start with more water than you actually need and let it simmer for about an hour so it reduces by half, which allows for its flavor to become more concentrated. This is a soup you'll continually season as you go, so have a tasting spoon ready. Because you're starting with water, don't be afraid to be generous with the salt—it can handle it.

To make the broth: Peel off the papery outer layers of the garlic heads, keeping just a few firm inner layers to keep the head intact. Cut off ¼ to ½ inch (0.6 to 1 cm) from the top of the heads, crosswise, to expose the cloves.

Heat the olive oil in a large Dutch oven over medium-low heat. Place the garlic heads, cut-side down, into the hot oil and sear until lightly golden brown, 7 to 10 minutes. Add the water, increase the heat to high, and bring to a boil.

Once boiling, reduce the heat to maintain a simmer and stir in the Parmesan rinds, sage, a few generous pinches of salt, several grinds of black pepper, and a generous pinch of red pepper flakes (if using). Simmer uncovered, stirring occasionally, until reduced by about half, 45 to 60 minutes.

Using a slotted spoon, remove and discard the garlic, Parmesan rinds, and sage sprigs. Taste and season with additional salt and pepper, as needed. (You'll likely need to add several more generous pinches of salt and a few more grinds of pepper.)

Continues >

Continued

To make the soup: Place 1 cup of white beans in a small bowl and mash with the back of a fork until a few lumps remain.

Stir the mashed white beans and remaining whole white beans into the broth and simmer for 10 minutes. Add the greens to the broth, handful by handful, followed by the lemon zest, and simmer until the greens are just wilted, about 1 minute. Remove the pot from the heat and stir in the lemon juice. Serve garnished with shaved Parmesan and, if desired, a pinch more red pepper flakes.

The Case for Saving Your Parmesan Rinds

We go through a lot of Parmesan at home. In fact, I can't actually remember a time when there wasn't a large chunk in the refrigerator. Because I always opt to buy whole pieces of Parmesan and grate them myself rather than pick up the pre-grated stuff, I am left with the hard rinds after I go through them. They're arguably the best part: They lend deep, rich flavor that's both savory and salty. Beyond this soup, try adding one or two to just about any other broth, soup, or sauce you make, and let them simmer with the rest of the ingredients.

When I've finished off a chunk of cheese, I toss the rind into a collection bag of spent rinds I keep in my freezer. They'll last for months there and can be tossed into the pot straight from the freezer. However, if I do run out, I've got the grocery store on backup. Stores like Whole Foods actually sell containers of Parmesan rinds leftover from cutting down a wheel—head to the cheese section and if you don't see them, just ask!

CHAPTER 4

Beans, Grains, and a Few Bready Things

What I love about things like beans, risotto, and even good toast, all of which are featured in this chapter, is their versatility. They're all such empty canvases that can be transformed into whatever you want them to be depending on what you add to them and how many mouths you want to feed. Sure, a slice of toast is more often thought of as a snack but pile it with one or two tasty things and suddenly it's a dead-simple dinner, too. Or stir lots of vegetables into a pot of cooked grains like farro and you've got something that's just as good at playing side dish as it is taking the role of a satisfying, albeit meatless, main. Eat these recipes as you like them, when you like them.

Olive Oil–Braised White Beans

2 (15-ounce, or 425 g) cans white beans, such as cannellini, drained and rinsed

6 garlic cloves, smashed and peeled

4 fresh sage leaves

Kosher salt

Freshly ground black pepper

Pinch red pepper flakes (optional)

¾ cup (180 ml) extra-virgin olive oil

1 teaspoon red wine vinegar

—

Serves 4 to 6

Although there's great reward in the time it takes to cook dried beans, there's just no arguing with the convenience of canned beans. I keep both stocked in my pantry but there's no doubt I go through the cans more quickly, even though they lack the same texture and flavor of dried. This, however, is one of my favorite ways to get canned beans tasting closer to the dried variety. Slowly braise a couple of cans of white beans in the oven, in olive oil that's been infused with lots of garlic and a few sage leaves, and they're transformed. The beans soak up the rich oil to become intensely creamy on the inside and deeply flavored. If you're not convinced that beans should be part of your regular routine, I think this recipe will persuade you.

—

How to serve these white beans? Start by bringing them to the table warm in their baking dish to spoon on top of thick-sliced toast as a humble, homey main dish. The next day, serve leftovers over greens, sliced tomatoes, or roasted vegetables for lunch or toss them with cooked brown rice for a simple grain salad. You can even purée what's left to use as a creamy sauce for pasta, thinning it as needed with a splash or two of pasta cooking water.

Place a rack in the middle of the oven and preheat the oven to 325°F (170°C).

Place the white beans, garlic, sage, ½ teaspoon of salt, several grinds of black pepper, and the red pepper flakes (if using), in a 9 × 13-inch (23 × 33 cm) baking dish or other 3-quart (3 L) baking dish. Pour in the olive oil and gently stir to combine.

Tightly cover the dish with aluminum foil and cook, stirring halfway through, until the white beans are soft but not falling apart and the mixture is bubbling, 35 to 40 minutes.

Stir in the vinegar and let cool for 5 minutes. Taste and season with additional salt and pepper, as needed. Serve warm or at room temperature.

Black Lentil Fritters with Lemon-Herb Yogurt

For Fritters:

1 cup (200 g) dried black lentils, picked over and rinsed

1 teaspoon kosher salt

⅔ cup (80 g) chickpea flour

1 garlic clove, grated or minced

½ teaspoon ground cumin

Freshly ground black pepper

¼ cup (60 ml) water

4 tablespoons (60 ml) extra-virgin olive oil, divided

For Lemon-Herb Yogurt:

1 cup (227 g) whole milk plain Greek yogurt

Finely grated zest of ½ lemon

Juice of ½ lemon

¼ cup (14 g) loosely packed finely chopped mixed fresh herbs, such as parsley, basil, cilantro, thyme, oregano, tarragon, and/or dill

¼ teaspoon kosher salt

Freshly ground black pepper

—

Serves 4

In college, when I tried to make lentils for the first time, I undercooked them so severely that I immediately wrote them off. When I finally got the courage to try again, I realized that, honestly, I just didn't really like lentils that much, even when they were properly cooked. Then one day I saw a recipe that called for black lentils and I was so taken by their striking, caviar-like appearance I was willing to give lentils another go. I am so glad I did because black lentils are truly the lentils for people who, like me, found all others to be a yawn. They cook quickly, hold their shape, and have an earthy, full-bodied flavor, almost like black beans.

—

I love to make these hearty, protein-packed fritters at the start of the week to pack up for easy lunches, or just to have on hand for a quick dinner. What's so magical about them is unlike other fritter recipes, eggs aren't used as a binder. Instead, when you mix chickpea flour with a bit of water, it becomes a sticky batter that holds together the cumin-spiced lentils.

To make the fritters: Place the lentils in a medium saucepan. Add enough water to cover the lentils by 1 inch (2.5 cm). Place the pot over high heat and bring to a boil. Reduce the heat and gently simmer until tender, about 20 minutes.

To make the lemon-herb yogurt: Meanwhile, in a medium bowl, combine all the yogurt ingredients, along with several grinds of black pepper, and mix well to combine. Set aside.

Continues >

Note:

I love the texture, flavor, and look of black lentils, but if you can't find them, green lentils—either French or regular—can be substituted.

Continued

To finish the fritters: When the lentils are cooked, drain them, transfer to a large bowl, and stir in the salt. Mash lightly with a fork, keeping about half the lentils whole. Let cool for 10 minutes.

Stir in the chickpea flour, garlic, cumin, and several grinds of black pepper. Drizzle in the water and stir to combine and form a sticky mixture. You should be able to a form a patty in your hands without it falling apart.

Heat 2 tablespoons (30 ml) of olive oil in a large cast iron or other heavy-bottomed skillet over medium-high heat. Drop 4 (¼-cup, or about 98 g) portions of batter into the skillet, flattening each gently with a spatula into roughly 3-inch (7.5 cm)-wide and ½-inch (1 cm)-thick fritters.

Pan-fry until a dark crust forms on the bottom, about 3 minutes. Flip the fritters and continue to cook until crisp on the other side, 2 to 3 minutes more. Transfer to a paper towel–lined plate.

Add the remaining 2 tablespoons (30 ml) of olive oil to the skillet and repeat with the remaining batter.

Serve warm or at room temperature, dolloped generously with the lemon-herb yogurt.

Note:

These fritters freeze well, stored in an airtight container or zip-top freezer bag, for a couple of months, so consider making a double batch if you have time. To reheat, don't worry about defrosting, just heat from frozen on a baking sheet in a 325°F (170°C) oven until warmed through.

Spicy Broccoli Rabe and Chickpea Skillet

2 tablespoons (30 ml) extra-virgin olive oil

2 (15-ounce, or 425 g) cans chickpeas, drained, rinsed, and patted dry

Kosher salt

2 large bunches (about 2 pounds, or 908 g, total) broccoli rabe, rinsed, stemmed, and cut into 2-inch (5 cm)-long pieces

¼ cup (60 ml) dry white wine, or water

3 garlic cloves, minced

Finely grated zest of ½ lemon

½ teaspoon red pepper flakes

Juice of ½ lemon

Freshly grated Pecorino Romano or Parmesan cheese, for serving (optional)

—

Serves 4

It's highly probable you'll grab the amount of broccoli rabe called for in this recipe at the grocery store and think I am crazy. Let me assure that while it may look like you're buying too much, you're not. Like all greens, broccoli rabe cooks down and shrinks quite a bit, but the hefty bunches can look intimidating at first. This quick beans-and-greens skillet is a light yet satisfying meatless main, though it can also be stretched and served as a side. Cooking the chickpeas in the hot skillet first gets them nice and crunchy, to provide contrast to the tender greens. Broccoli rabe is inherently bitter and it does still have a bite here, but the acid from both the white wine and lemon juice, along with garlic and the kick of red pepper flakes, do help put it in its place.

Heat the olive oil in large skillet over medium-high heat. Add the chickpeas in a single layer and season with ¼ teaspoon of salt. Cook for about 1 minute until lightly browned in spots on the bottom. Stir and continue to cook, stirring occasionally, until crispy and lightly browned in spots all over, 4 to 5 minutes more. Transfer to a large plate or bowl.

Add the broccoli rabe to the skillet in handfuls and sauté until it just starts to wilt and you can fit it all in the skillet. Reduce the heat to medium-low. Pour in the white wine, cover the skillet, and simmer, stirring every so often, until almost all the wine has evaporated and the broccoli rabe is tender, about 5 minutes.

Add the garlic, lemon zest, remaining ½ teaspoon of salt, and red pepper flakes. Sauté until fragrant, about 1 minute. Remove from the heat and stir in the chickpeas and lemon juice. Taste and season with additional salt as needed. Serve garnished with grated cheese, if desired.

Chickpea Flatbread with Whipped Feta and Marinated Tomatoes

For Flatbread:

1 cup (120 g) chickpea flour

1 cup (240 ml) water

3 tablespoons (45 ml) extra-virgin olive oil, divided

½ teaspoon kosher salt

1 small garlic clove, grated or minced

For Marinated Tomatoes:

1 pint (about 2 cups, or 300 g), cherry tomatoes, or grape tomatoes halved

1 teaspoon extra-virgin olive oil

1 teaspoon sherry vinegar, or red wine vinegar

½ teaspoon chopped fresh oregano

Kosher salt

Freshly ground black pepper

For Whipped Feta:

4 ounces (113 g) feta cheese, crumbled (about 1 cup)

2 tablespoons (28 g) whole milk plain Greek yogurt

—

Serves 2 to 4

When you combine chickpea flour with water to form a golden yellow batter and bake it, the result is a gluten-free, protein-rich flatbread that's all too easy to snack on. It's addictive on its own (see Cacio e Pepe Farinata, page 42) but also happens to be sturdy enough for toppings. Here I use it as a vehicle for feta cheese that's been whipped to impossible creaminess. (Spreading it on the flatbread keeps my temptation simply to eat it straight from the food processor at bay!) Quickly marinating the tomatoes while you work on the rest of the recipe allows some of their sweet juices to release so they become their best selves. You can marinate the tomatoes in either sherry vinegar or red wine vinegar, depending on what you have on hand, though I especially love the nutty sweetness of sherry vinegar.

To make the flatbread: In a medium bowl, whisk the chickpea flour, water, 1 tablespoon (15 ml) of olive oil, and salt until smooth. Cover and let the mixture rest at room temperature to give the flour time to absorb the water, at least 30 minutes, or up to 2 hours. Meanwhile, make the marinated tomatoes and whipped feta.

To make the marinated tomatoes: In a medium bowl, combine the tomatoes, olive oil, vinegar, oregano, a pinch of salt, and a few grinds of black pepper. Set aside.

To make the whipped feta: Place the feta in the bowl of a food processor fitted with the blade attachment. Pulse into small crumbs, about 6 to 8 pulses. Add the yogurt and blend, stopping to scrape down the sides of the bowl as needed, until the mixture is whipped and very smooth, about 2 minutes. Transfer to a small bowl and set aside. If not using immediately, cover and refrigerate.

Continues >

Continued

To cook the flatbread and assemble: Place a rack in the top third of the oven (6 to 8 inches, or 15 to 20 cm, from the broiling element) and preheat the oven to 450°F (230°C). You want to get the entire oven nice and hot before broiling the flatbread, so it bakes evenly.

Place a 10-inch (25 cm) cast iron skillet in the oven and turn on the broiler. Let it sit under the broiler for 5 minutes.

Do your best to skim off and discard most of the foam that has formed on the surface of the chickpea flour batter. Stir the garlic into the batter.

Carefully remove the hot skillet from the oven. Add the remaining 2 table-spoons (30 ml) of olive oil and carefully swirl to coat the bottom of the skillet. Pour the batter into the skillet and return it to the oven. Broil until the edges of the flatbread are set, the center is firm, and the top is lightly browned in spots, 6 to 10 minutes. Remove from the oven. Let cool for 5 minutes, then carefully slide a flat spatula under the flatbread and transfer it to a cutting board.

Spread the whipped feta on top, leaving a border around the edges. Using a slotted spoon, scoop out the marinated tomatoes and pile them over the feta. Garnish with a few grinds of pepper. Use a knife or pizza cutter to slice the flatbread into quarters and serve.

Cheesy Brussels Sprout and Farro Bake

2 tablespoons (30 ml) extra-virgin olive oil, plus more for coating the dish

Kosher salt

1 cup (200 g) farro, rinsed and drained (see page 95)

1 pound (454 g) Brussels sprouts, stem ends trimmed

1 tablespoon (15 ml) balsamic vinegar

2 teaspoons Dijon mustard (smooth, whole grain, or a combination)

Freshly ground black pepper

4 ounces (113 g) Gruyère cheese, grated (about 1 cup)

½ cup (70 g) hazelnuts, toasted and chopped

½ cup (28 g) packed fresh finely grated Parmesan cheese

Coarsely chopped fresh parsley, for serving (optional)

—

Serves 4 to 6

Maybe because I grew up on them (like so many of us did), I have a soft spot for casseroles, even though they're hardly trendy these days. So, I am calling this a "bake" to keep up with the times, but truly, it's the most delightful casserole I've eaten in years. Or, should I say, it's a bit like a warm grain salad that's held together with lots of melty Gruyère cheese and made browned and crisp on top with Parmesan. Toasted hazelnuts add crunch and balsamic and Dijon provide the right amount of tang to prevent each bite from feeling heavy. Eat it as a main dish or side dish, whichever you prefer. I also happen to think it can be quite a star at the Thanksgiving table. And if you have any leftover, don't sleep on it; It's one of my favorite lunches, eaten warm, at room temperature, or cold.

Place a rack in the top third of the oven (6 to 8 inches, or 15 to 20 cm, from the broiling element) and preheat the oven to 400°F (200°C). Coat a 9 × 13-inch (23 × 33 cm) or other 3-quart (3 L) baking dish with olive oil. Set aside.

Bring a large pot of salted water to a boil over high heat. Add the farro to the boiling water and cook until al dente (it should be tender but have a slight chew in the center), 25 to 30 minutes.

Meanwhile, thinly slice the Brussels sprouts with a knife, a mandoline, or the slicing blade of a food processor and place them in a large bowl.

When the farro is ready, drain well and return it to the pot off the heat. Cover and set aside to steam for 10 minutes, then transfer to the bowl of Brussels sprouts.

Add ¼ teaspoon of salt, the olive oil, vinegar, Dijon, and several grinds of black pepper. Toss to combine. Stir in the Gruyère and hazelnuts. Taste and season with additional salt and pepper, as needed.

Continues >

Continued

Transfer the farro mixture to the prepared baking dish and spread it into an even layer. Sprinkle the Parmesan evenly over the top.

Loosely cover the dish with aluminum foil and bake for 20 minutes. Remove the foil, turn on the broiler, and broil until the Parmesan softens and browns, 4 to 5 minutes. Let cool for 5 minutes and sprinkle with parsley, if desired, before serving.

What, Exactly, is Farro?

When I was living in Italy, I craved the nutty, wholesomeness of brown rice, and yet I just couldn't find it at my corner grocery store. Instead, my choices were risotto rice or farro. So, farro and I became fast friends. Farro is an ancient whole grain that's gained popularity over the past handful of years, but if you're not yet familiar with it, here are the facts: It's got a similar flavor to brown rice but with a heartier, chewier texture. Like all whole grains, it's high in fiber but with the added benefit of being high in protein, too. Oh, and if gluten is a concern, it's important to know that farro is derived from wheat, so it is not gluten-free, however being that it's an ancient grain, it hasn't been as processed over the years as regular wheat, so those with a mild sensitively may find they can tolerate it.

One thing to pay attention to: Farro is sold in a few forms. You'll find whole, semi-pearled, and pearled, the latter two meaning part or all of the exterior bran has been removed so the farro cooks more quickly. What's confusing is that the form is not always clearly labeled on the package. However, if the instructions on the package list a 10- to 15-minute cook time, it's probably pearled, unless, to make the whole matter more complicated, it's par-cooked, which both Trader Joe's and Whole Foods sell in small bags. If it says 25 to 30 minutes, it's likely semi-pearled, and if it requires overnight soaking or states a cook time of 1 hour or more, it's whole. This recipe follows the cooking time for semi-pearled farro, which I find to be the most common variety on grocery store shelves—Bob's Red Mill and Rustichella d'Abruzzo are two easy-to-find brands, though because things weren't already muddled enough, Rustichella d'Abruzzo labels their farro as "whole" even though it's semi-pearled. All this to say, you can really use whichever type of farro you find and prefer for this recipe. However, if the cook time on the package is different from what I've noted in the recipe, follow what the package states instead.

No-Fail Parmesan Risotto

6 cups (1.5 L) low-sodium chicken broth, or vegetable broth

1 tablespoon (15 ml) extra-virgin olive oil

1 shallot, finely chopped

Kosher salt

Freshly ground black pepper

1½ cups (300 g) carnaroli, arborio, or vialone nano rice (see page 98)

½ cup (120 ml) dry white wine

½ cup (28 g) packed fresh finely grated Parmesan cheese, plus more for serving

1 tablespoon (14 g) unsalted butter

—

Serves 4

Risotto has a reputation for being fussy, which I was convinced of until I got the hang of making it. Once I did, I quickly realized it's not much harder than boiling a pot of pasta, aside from the frequent stirring. This basic recipe is guaranteed to set you up for success and give you the confidence to make risotto a part of your everyday dinners. Cook this classic version first, to get the hang of when to add each ingredient and to understand the visual cues that signify perfectly creamy end results, then jump to the four seasonal variations that follow. Because this base recipe is plain and simple, I like to use it as a bed for things like Rosemary Brown Butter Scallops (page 163), Shrimp Scampi over Polenta (page 107), and Skillet Lemon Chicken Thighs with Blistered Olives (page 164). The four variations, however, are fortified with enough vegetables and other good things that they can stand alone for dinner.

Place the broth in a medium saucepan and bring to a simmer over medium heat. Reduce the heat to low and keep warm.

Heat the olive oil in a large, high-sided sauté pan or Dutch oven over medium heat. Add the shallot, a generous pinch of salt, and a few grinds of black pepper. Sauté until softened and fragrant, about 2 minutes.

Add the rice and cook, stirring, until the edges have turned translucent but the center is still opaque and the grains smells lightly toasted, about 2 minutes.

Pour in the wine and simmer, stirring constantly, until the wine has evaporated and the pan is almost dry, about 1 minute.

Continues >

Continued

Add the warm broth, 1 ladleful at a time, stirring constantly. Wait to add another ladleful until the liquid has been almost completely absorbed by the rice. Begin tasting the rice after about 12 minutes to gauge how far it has cooked. At this point, stir in another generous pinch of salt and a few more grinds of black pepper.

Continue adding the broth until the rice is al dente and the broth is creamy. The risotto is done when the rice is tender but still has a bit of chew, the texture is of a thick porridge, and, if you run your spatula through it, it will slowly fill in the space, 20 to 30 minutes total (you might not use all the broth).

Remove the pan from the heat. Stir in the cheese and butter. Taste and season with additional salt and pepper, as needed. (I usually add another generous pinch of salt and a bit more black pepper.) Serve immediately.

All About Risotto Rice

There are a few types of rice commonly used to make risotto, and, though they all successfully achieve the end result, they do so a touch differently. Arborio is perhaps the most common risotto rice available and although it's the one I used when I first starting cooking risotto—because it's the easiest to find—it's now not the one I prefer. Arborio is a great choice if that's what you can easily get your hands on, but I find carnaroli to be the most forgiving. Whereas arborio can go from perfectly creamy to gummy in seconds, carnaroli is hard to overcook, making it the ultimate choice for risotto beginners and those who prefer consistency alike. Vialone nano is one more good choice that's a little harder to find but it holds its shape well and is a little less starchy, producing a risotto that's a bit lighter in body but still creamy.

SUMMER
Fresh Corn and Tomato Risotto

2 ears sweet corn, shucked, kernels removed, and cobs reserved

6 cups (1.5 L) low-sodium chicken broth, or vegetable broth

1 tablespoon (15 ml) extra-virgin olive oil

1 shallot, finely chopped

Kosher salt

Freshly ground black pepper

1½ cups (300 g) carnaroli, arborio, or vialone nano rice

½ cup (120 ml) dry white wine

2 tomatoes, chopped

½ cup (28 g) packed fresh finely grated Parmesan cheese, plus more for serving

1 tablespoon (14 g) unsalted butter

¼ cup (10 g) loosely packed chopped fresh basil leaves

—

Serves 4

What's ingenious about this recipe is that the corncobs aren't immediately discarded after the kernels are cut off them. Instead, toss them into the pot while you warm the broth and they'll infuse the broth with so much sweet corn flavor that the resulting risotto tastes even more deeply of this summer favorite.

Break the reserved corncobs in half crosswise with your hands and place them in a medium saucepan. Pour in the broth and bring to a simmer over medium heat. Reduce the heat to low and keep warm.

Heat the olive oil in a large, high-sided sauté pan or Dutch oven over medium heat. Add the shallot, a generous pinch of salt, and a few grinds of black pepper. Sauté until softened and fragrant, about 2 minutes.

Add the rice and cook, stirring, until the edges have turned translucent but the center is still opaque and the grains smells lightly toasted, about 2 minutes.

Pour in the wine and simmer, stirring constantly, until the wine has evaporated and the pan is almost dry, about 1 minute.

Add the warm broth, 1 ladleful at a time, stirring constantly. Wait to add another ladleful until the liquid has been almost completely absorbed by the rice. Begin tasting the rice after about 12 minutes to gauge how far it has cooked. At this point, stir in the corn kernels and tomatoes, along with another generous pinch of salt, and a few more grinds of black pepper.

Continue adding broth until the rice is al dente and the broth is creamy. The tomatoes will begin to release their juices, so you might pause adding broth until the rice soaks up some of these juices. The risotto is done when the rice is tender but still has a bit of chew, the texture is of a thick porridge, and, if you run your spatula through it, it will slowly fill in the space, 20 to 30 minutes total (you might not use all the broth).

Remove the pan from the heat. Stir in the cheese and butter. Taste and season with additional salt and pepper, as needed. (I usually add another generous pinch of salt and a bit more black pepper.) Stir in the basil and serve immediately, garnishing each bowl with additional grated Parmesan.

FALL
Sweet Potato and Sage Risotto

6 cups (1.5 L) low-sodium chicken broth, or vegetable broth

3 tablespoons (45 ml) extra-virgin olive oil, divided

12 fresh sage leaves

1 large (about 12 ounces, or 340 g) sweet potato, cut into ¼-inch (0.6 cm) chunks

1 shallot, finely chopped

Kosher salt

Freshly ground black pepper

1½ cups (300 g) carnaroli, arborio, or vialone nano rice

½ cup (120 ml) dry white wine

4 ounces (113 g) Fontina cheese, grated (about 1 cup)

1 tablespoon (14 g) unsalted butter

—

Serves 4

Although it's easy enough to stir chopped sage into risotto to flavor it, it's a whole lot more fun to pan-fry leaves so they become chip-like and can be crumbled on top of each bowl to lend a bit of crunch. Swap out the usual Parmesan for buttery, extra-melty Fontina cheese, which cozies up well to the tender chunks of sweet potatoes, and you've got the perfect fall dinner to sink into.

Place the broth in a medium saucepan and bring to a simmer over medium heat. Reduce the heat to low and keep warm.

Heat the olive oil in a large, high-sided sauté pan or Dutch oven over medium-high heat. Add the sage leaves and cook until crisp, about 30 seconds. Using tongs or a slotted spoon, carefully transfer to a paper towel–lined plate.

Reduce the heat to medium. Add the sweet potato, shallot, a generous pinch of salt, and a few grinds of black pepper. Sauté until the sweet potato begins to brown and the shallot is softened and fragrant, about 2 minutes.

Add the rice and cook, stirring, until the edges have turned translucent but the center is still opaque and the grains smells lightly toasted, about 2 minutes.

Pour in the wine and simmer, stirring constantly, until the wine has evaporated and the pan is almost dry, about 1 minute.

Add the warm broth, 1 ladleful at a time, stirring constantly. Wait to add another ladleful until the liquid has been almost completely absorbed by the rice. Begin tasting the rice after about 12 minutes to gauge how far it has cooked. At this point, stir in another generous pinch of salt and a few more grinds of black pepper.

Continue adding broth until the rice is al dente and the broth is creamy. The risotto is done when the sweet potato is tender, the rice is tender but still has a bit of chew, the texture is of a thick porridge, and, if you run your spatula through it, it will slowly fill in the space, 20 to 30 minutes total (you might not use all the broth).

Remove the pan from the heat. Stir in the cheese and butter. Reserve 8 whole crispy sage leaves, then break the remaining into small pieces with your hands and stir them into the risotto. Taste and season with additional salt and pepper, as needed. (I usually add another generous pinch of salt and a bit more black pepper.) Serve immediately, garnishing each bowl with the reserved sage leaves.

WINTER
Mushroom and Radicchio Risotto

6 cups (1.5 L) low-sodium chicken broth, or vegetable broth

3 tablespoons (45 ml) extra-virgin olive oil, divided

1 pound (454 g) cremini mushrooms, sliced

Kosher salt

Freshly ground black pepper

1 shallot, finely chopped

1½ cups (300 g) carnaroli, arborio, or vialone nano rice

½ cup (120 ml) dry white wine

1 small head (about 6 ounces, or 170 g) radicchio, cored, quartered, and cut crosswise into ½-inch (1 cm)-wide strips (about 3 cups)

½ cup (28 g) packed fresh finely grated Pecorino Romano cheese, plus more for serving

1 tablespoon (14 g) unsalted butter

—

Serves 4

Wilted leaves of radicchio lend a pale-purple hue to this nourishing cold-weather risotto. Earthy mushrooms hold their own next to the leaves' natural bitterness, though stirring the radicchio into the bubbling pan of risotto and smothering it in salty, pungent Pecorino most definitely allows it to mellow.

Place the broth in a medium saucepan and bring to a simmer over medium heat. Reduce the heat to low and keep warm.

Heat 2 tablespoons (30 ml) of olive oil in a large, high-sided sauté pan or Dutch oven over medium heat. Add the mushrooms, season with salt and pepper, and cook, stirring occasionally, until the mushrooms are browned and tender, about 5 minutes. Transfer to a plate.

Pour the remaining 1 tablespoon (15 ml) of olive oil into the pan. Add the shallot, a generous pinch of salt, and a few grinds of black pepper. Sauté until softened and fragrant, about 2 minutes.

Add the rice and cook, stirring, until the edges have turned translucent but the center is still opaque and the grains smells lightly toasted, about 2 minutes.

Pour in the wine and simmer, stirring constantly, until the wine has evaporated and the pan is almost dry, about 1 minute.

Add the warm broth, 1 ladleful at a time, stirring constantly. Wait to add another ladleful until the liquid has been almost completely absorbed by the rice. Begin tasting the rice after about 12 minutes to gauge how far it has cooked. At this point, stir in the radicchio and sautéed mushrooms, along with another generous pinch of salt and a few more grinds of black pepper.

Continue adding broth until the rice is al dente and the broth is creamy. The risotto is done when the radicchio is wilted, the rice is tender but still has a bit of chew, the texture is of a thick porridge, and, if you run your spatula through it, it will slowly fill in the space, 20 to 30 minutes total (you might not use all the broth).

Remove the pan from the heat. Stir in the cheese and butter. Taste and season with additional salt and pepper, as needed. (I usually add another generous pinch of salt and a bit more black pepper.) Serve immediately, garnishing each bowl with additional grated Pecorino.

SPRING
Lemony Asparagus Risotto

When it's peak asparagus season, you hardly need to do much to show off the vibrant green, grassy stalks. Pair them with plenty of bright lemon zest and juice and you've got a risotto that tastes like the first sunny days of spring.

6 cups (1.5 L) low-sodium chicken broth, or vegetable broth

1 tablespoon (15 ml) extra-virgin olive oil

1 leek, white and light green parts only, cleaned and chopped

Kosher salt

Freshly ground black pepper

1½ cups (300 g) carnaroli, arborio, or vialone nano rice

½ cup (120 ml) dry white wine

1 pound (454 g) asparagus, woody ends trimmed, cut into 1-inch (2.5 cm) pieces on the bias

Finely grated zest of 1 lemon

½ cup (28 g) packed fresh finely grated Parmesan cheese, plus more for serving

1 tablespoon (14 g) unsalted butter

Juice of 1 lemon

—

Serves 4

Place the broth in a medium saucepan and bring to a simmer over medium heat. Reduce the heat to low and keep warm.

Heat the olive oil in a large, high-sided sauté pan or Dutch oven over medium heat. Add the leek, a generous pinch of salt, and a few grinds of black pepper. Sauté until softened and fragrant, about 4 minutes.

Add the rice and cook, stirring, until the edges have turned translucent but the center is still opaque and the grains smells lightly toasted, about 2 minutes.

Pour in the wine and simmer, stirring constantly, until the wine has evaporated and the pan is almost dry, about 1 minute.

Add the warm broth, 1 ladleful at a time, stirring constantly. Wait to add another ladleful until the liquid has been almost completely absorbed by the rice. Begin tasting the rice after about 12 minutes to gauge how far it has cooked. At this point, stir in the asparagus and lemon zest, along with another generous pinch of salt and a few more grinds of black pepper.

Continue adding broth until the rice is al dente and the broth is creamy. The risotto is done when the asparagus is bright green and tender, the rice is tender but still has a bit of chew, the texture is of a thick porridge, and, if you run your spatula through it, it will slowly fill in the space, 20 to 30 minutes total (you might not use all the broth).

Remove the pan from the heat. Stir in the cheese, butter, and lemon juice. Taste and season with additional salt and pepper, as needed. (I usually add another generous pinch of salt and a bit more black pepper.) Serve immediately, garnishing each bowl with additional grated Parmesan.

Creamy Oven Polenta

Extra-virgin olive oil, for coating the dish

1 cup (163 g) polenta (coarse-ground, not instant or quick-cooking)

1 teaspoon kosher salt

Freshly ground black pepper

4 cups (1 L) water

½ cup (28 g) packed fresh finely grated Parmesan cheese

2 tablespoons (28 g) unsalted butter, cubed

—

Serves 4

Without a doubt, this is the easiest, most foolproof way to cook polenta. For years, I labored over the traditional stovetop approach, and for every time it came out perfectly, there were at least a couple times it would end up gummy and cement-like. Cooking polenta in the oven isn't conventional but it's the only method I've found that produces the most consistent results. It also happens to be the most hands-off approach: Slip a baking dish of polenta and water in the oven and return less than an hour later to find perfectly creamy results—no standing over the pot, stirring, required.

—

This polenta is a complete blank slate, so what follows are three toppings that turn the comforting porridge into dinner. While the polenta does its thing in the oven, focus your energy on making the topping of your choice on the stove.

Place a rack in the middle of the oven and preheat the oven to 350°F (180°C). Drizzle a bit of olive oil into an 8 × 8-inch (20 × 20 cm) or other 2-quart (2 L) baking dish and use your hands to coat the bottom and sides of the dish with oil.

Add the polenta, salt, and several grinds of black pepper to the dish. Pour in the water and whisk to combine.

Bake, uncovered, for 40 minutes. Remove from the oven and whisk in the cheese and butter cubes (the butter doesn't need to be completely melted).

Return to the oven and bake, uncovered, until all the liquid is absorbed and the polenta is creamy, 8 to 10 minutes more. Whisk once or twice more and serve immediately with the topping of your choice.

Shopping for Polenta

It's important to use the right type of polenta here, but I'll be honest, shopping for it can be unnecessarily complicated if you don't know what you're looking for. Bypass instant or quick cooking polenta, as well as the pre-cooked tubes. Instead, look for coarse-ground polenta. It's easy to find at Italian markets but if you're shopping for it at larger grocery stores, Bob's Red Mill is likely to be the brand you'll come across, although they confusingly label their polenta as "Corn Grits Polenta."

Quick Sausage Ragù over Polenta

1 (28-ounce, or 794 g) can whole peeled tomatoes

2 tablespoons (30 ml) extra-virgin olive oil

1 pound (454 g) hot Italian sausage, or sweet Italian sausage (chicken, turkey, or pork), casings removed if using links

1 medium yellow onion, finely chopped

2 garlic cloves, minced

2 tablespoons (32 g) tomato paste

1 rosemary sprig

Kosher salt

Freshly ground black pepper

1 tablespoon (15 ml) balsamic vinegar

¼ cup (10 g) loosely packed chopped fresh basil leaves

1 batch Creamy Oven Polenta (page 105)

Freshly grated Parmesan cheese, for serving (optional)

—

Serves 4

Although it's hard to beat the depth of flavor that comes from a slow-simmered ragù, I think this one comes close. That's thanks to a couple of key ingredients. Starting with sausage instead of ground meat gives you a jump-start, as it's already packed with seasoning. Perhaps even more important, though, is the balsamic vinegar. Stirring in a spoonful at the end of cooking lends a richness to the dish that's hard to pinpoint, but you may fool everyone into thinking this sat on the stove a whole lot longer than it actually did.

Empty the canned tomatoes with their juices into a large bowl and carefully crush them with hands (you'll have some bite-size pieces remaining). Set aside.

Heat the olive oil in a large, high-sided sauté pan or skillet over medium-high heat. Add the sausage and cook , breaking it up into bite-size pieces with a wooden spoon, until browned, about 5 minutes. (It will not be completely cooked through just yet.)

Reduce the heat to medium. Add the onion and cook, stirring occasionally until softened and translucent, 3 to 5 minutes. Add the garlic and tomato paste. Sauté until fragrant and the tomato paste has slightly darkened in color, about 1 minute.

Carefully pour the crushed tomatoes into the skillet. Stir in the rosemary, a generous pinch of salt, and several grinds of black pepper. Bring to a simmer and cook, uncovered, until the sauce has thickened slightly, about 10 minutes.

Remove from the heat, and remove and discard the rosemary sprig. Stir in the vinegar and basil. Taste and season with additional salt and pepper, as needed. Serve over the polenta and garnish with grated Parmesan, if desired.

Shrimp Scampi over Polenta

1 pound (454 g) uncooked medium peeled and deveined shrimp

Kosher salt

Freshly ground black pepper

2 tablespoons (30 ml) extra-virgin olive oil

4 garlic cloves, thinly sliced

¼ teaspoon red pepper flakes

½ cup (120 ml) dry white wine

3 tablespoons (42 g) unsalted butter, cubed

¼ cup (10 g) loosely packed chopped fresh parsley

Juice of ½ lemon

1 batch Creamy Oven Polenta (page 105)

———

Serves 4

Shrimp scampi is just about the fastest, fanciest thing you can make in your kitchen. There's something about shrimp swimming in a garlicky butter sauce that feels luxurious, and yet it only takes about 5 minutes to pull together. Because it does cook so quickly and is best enjoyed immediately, wait until you've added the cheese and butter to the polenta and returned it to the oven to prepare the shrimp.

Pat the shrimp dry with paper towels and season generously with salt and pepper. Set aside.

Heat the olive oil in a large skillet over medium heat. Add the garlic and red pepper flakes and sauté until fragrant and the garlic has softened and is only just beginning to turn light golden (you don't want it to brown), 1 to 2 minutes.

Add the shrimp in an even layer and cook, undisturbed, for 1 minute.

Flip the shrimp and pour in the wine. Cook until the shrimp are pink and opaque, and the wine has reduced slightly, 1 to 2 minutes.

Remove the skillet from the heat. Add the butter and stir until melted. Add the parsley and lemon juice, toss to combine, and serve over the polenta.

White Bean Ratatouille over Polenta

You'll make more of this colorful stew than you need for the polenta but that's actually intentional because this is one of those dishes that's even better the second day. I've been known to eat it cold out of the fridge for lunch (sometimes piled on toast, other times simply with a fork), or it can be folded into scrambled eggs or tossed with pasta to turn it into a whole new meal.

4 tablespoons (60 ml) extra-virgin olive oil, divided

1 medium eggplant (about 1 pound, or 454 g), cut into ½-inch (1 cm) chunks

Kosher salt

Freshly ground black pepper

2 medium zucchini, summer squash, or a combination (about 1 pound, or 454 g, total), cut into ½-inch (1 cm) chunks

1 medium red bell pepper (about 8 ounces, or 225 g), cut into ½-inch (1 cm) chunks

1 small yellow onion, finely chopped

1 pint (about 2 cups, or 300 g) cherry tomatoes, halved

2 garlic cloves, minced

2 teaspoons fresh thyme leaves

1 (15-ounce, or 425 g) can white beans, drained and rinsed

¼ cup (10 g) loosely packed chopped fresh basil leaves

1 batch Creamy Oven Polenta (page 105)

—

Serves 4 to 6

Heat 2 tablespoons (30 ml) of olive oil in a large, high-sided sauté pan or Dutch oven over medium-high heat. Add the eggplant and season with ½ teaspoon of salt and several grinds of black pepper. Cook, stirring occasionally, until browned in spots but not completely tender, about 2 minutes. Transfer to a large bowl.

Pour 1 tablespoon (15 ml) of olive oil into the pan. Add the zucchini, season with ½ teaspoon of salt and several grinds of black pepper, and cook, stirring occasionally, until browned in spots but not completely tender, about 2 minutes. Transfer to the bowl with the eggplant.

Reduce the heat to medium and pour the remaining 1 tablespoon (15 ml) of olive oil into the pan. Add the red bell pepper and onion, season with ¼ teaspoon of salt and a few grinds of black pepper, and sauté until the onion is softened and translucent, about 5 minutes. Add the tomatoes, garlic, and thyme and sauté for 1 minute more. Stir in the white beans, eggplant, and zucchini.

Cover the pan, reduce the heat to medium-low, and simmer, stirring occasionally, for 20 minutes. Remove from the heat and let cool, uncovered, for 10 minutes. Taste and season with additional salt and pepper, as needed. Stir in basil and serve over the polenta.

Whole-Wheat Skillet Focaccia

2 cups (256 g) all-purpose flour

1 cup (128 g) whole-wheat flour

1½ teaspoons kosher salt

1 teaspoon instant yeast

1¼ cups (300 ml) lukewarm water

4 tablespoons (60 ml) extra-virgin olive oil, divided

1 tablespoon (3 g) coarsely chopped fresh rosemary leaves

Flaky sea salt

—

Serves 8 to 10

If you've always wanted to make homemade bread but have been over-whelmed by the idea, start here. Focaccia is the most beginner-friendly bread there is and this one is infinitely so. That's because all that's required of you is to stir a few things together in a bowl. Let this tousled dough rest for a couple of hours, then toss it in the fridge to rest some more. Although most bread recipes come with a strict timetable, this one doesn't. Leave it in the fridge for as little as 8 hours and as long as 48—it will be ready and waiting for you.

—

The addition of whole-wheat flour to this focaccia lends a mildly nutty flavor and makes it a touch more wholesome, while still being so perfectly fluffy and olive oil rich. It's also impressively tall and thick, making it the perfect contender for slicing and using for sandwiches, too.

In a large bowl, stir together the all-purpose flour, whole-wheat flour, kosher salt, and yeast to combine. Add the water and 2 tablespoons (30 ml) of olive oil and stir until a shaggy dough forms. Using your hands, knead the dough a few times to ensure no dry flour remains and form it into a rough ball. Cover the bowl tightly with plastic wrap. (*Note: If the plastic wrap doesn't adhere well to the bowl you're using, use an elastic band to ensure it's tightly sealed.*) Let rest at room temperature for 2 hours.

After 2 hours, transfer the bowl of dough to the refrigerator and chill for at least 8 hours and up to 48.

When ready to bake, preheat the oven to 425°F (220°C). Drizzle 1 table-spoon (15 ml) of olive oil into a 10- or 12-inch (25 or 30 cm) cast iron or other oven-safe skillet.

Continues >

Note:

You can also bake the focaccia in an 8- or 9-inch (20 or 23 cm) round cake pan or 8-inch (20 cm) square baking pan.

Continued

Remove the bowl of dough from the refrigerator and use your hands to transfer the dough to the prepared skillet. Turn to coat the dough in the oil, then gently flatten it into a round disk, about 1 inch (2.5 cm) thick. The dough will not reach the edges of the skillet. Cover the skillet with plastic wrap and let rest for 10 minutes.

Using your hands, gently stretch the dough all the way to the edges of the skillet. Cover and let rest until puffed and slightly risen, 20 to 25 minutes more.

Press your fingertips firmly into the dough, pushing straight down to the bottom of the pan, in random spots to dimple the surface all over. Drizzle the remaining 1 tablespoon (15 ml) of olive oil over the dough so it pools in some of the indentations. Sprinkle with rosemary and a generous pinch of flaky sea salt.

Bake the focaccia until lightly golden brown, 20 to 25 minutes. Transfer the skillet to a wire cooling rack and let the focaccia cool for 10 to 15 minutes before slicing into it straight from the skillet, or sliding a flat spatula underneath and transferring it to a cutting board. Focaccia is best eaten warm, but it is also good at room temperature. If the crust gets too soft, reheat it in a 350°F (180°C) oven to crisp it up.

Note:

Although this focaccia is best served fresh, it also freezes like a dream. Slice it, slip into a zip-top freezer bag or airtight container, and toss it in the freezer for up to 1 or 2 months. When you need it, grab a wedge or two, let it defrost at room temperature, and then reheat it in a 350°F (180°C) oven until warmed through.

A Few Topping Suggestions

Fresh rosemary is a classic topping for focaccia, but it's really just the beginning. Once you've gotten comfortable with this recipe, I encourage you to experiment. Here are a handful of my favorite toppings. Try them alone or feel free to mix and match:

- *Any other hard herb, like oregano or thyme*
- *Roasted Garlic (page 30) cloves or thin roasted red onion wedges*
- *Thinly sliced lemon wheels*
- *Seeds like cumin, fennel, poppy, or sesame*
- *Pitted, coarsely chopped olives*
- *Spice blends like dukkah, za'atar, or even everything bagel seasoning*
- *Grated or crumbled cheese like Parmesan, Gruyère, or blue (sprinkle on halfway through to prevent the cheese from burning)*

Mozzarella Anchovy Toast

1 thick slice good sourdough
bread, or country-style bread

2 or 3 slices fresh mozzarella
cheese

1 or 2 oil-packed anchovy fillets,
drained

Freshly ground black pepper

—

Serves 1, but multiplies easily

There's a shoebox-size wine bar in Florence called Il Santino *that's one of my very favorite spots in the city. My husband, Joe, and I typically squeeze in at the bar, then order a bottle of wine and a slew of small plates, one of which is always the* crostone mozzarella e acciughe, *a simple toast topped with melted mozzarella and anchovy fillets. The combination of melted cheese and crusty bread is total Italian comfort food, and although whole anchovy fillets threw us a bit the first time we ordered it, they actually seal the deal. I know anchovies are a polarizing ingredient, but hear me out: They add a salty, umami element that really does make it all too easy to go in for another bite. Because we can't fly off to Florence every time we crave it, we now make the toast ourselves at home, enjoying it on its own as a snack or making a few toasts and pairing it with The Easiest Arugula Salad (page 72) for a light, barely cooked dinner. It manages to whisk us back to that little bar every time.*

Preheat the broiler.

Top the bread with the mozzarella and place it on a baking sheet. Broil until the cheese is melted and bubbly, about 5 minutes.

Place 1 or 2 anchovy fillets on top, finish with a few grinds of black pepper, and serve.

Tomato Bread with Burrata and Salsa Verde

4 thick slices good sourdough
bread, or country-style bread

1 garlic clove, peeled

1 large ripe tomato, halved

1 (8-ounce, or 225 g) ball
burrata cheese

Salsa Verde (page 25), for
serving

Flaky sea salt

Freshly ground black pepper

—

Serves 2 to 4

I pretty much don't need anything but a spoon to enjoy the intensely rich, almost buttery goodness that is burrata, but I tend to save that for when no one is watching. Here's a more civilized approach: Rub garlic and tomato all over thick-cut toast, pile it with burrata, and finish it off with a generous drizzle of garlicky, herby Salsa Verde. It's a little messy but, as you'll quickly realize when you go to grab a napkin, 100 percent worth it. Enjoy these bruschetta-like toasts as a snack or, my preference, as an unfussy, not-too-heavy lunch or dinner.

Lightly toast the bread slices. Rub the garlic clove all over one side of each toast, followed by the tomato halves. Squeeze and put pressure on the tomatoes, letting the seeds and juice fall on the toast.

Tear the burrata and divide the pieces among the toast. Spoon salsa verde over the top and serve with a sprinkle of salt and a couple of grinds of black pepper.

The 3-Step Trick to Perfect Pasta

Maybe you've wondered why pasta dishes you order at good Italian restaurants are just a little bit better than the ones you cook at home. How is it that the pasta is both perfectly cooked and married to the sauce? This is because they lean on a simple 3-step trick. I use it in almost all the recipes in this chapter, aside from those where the sauce isn't cooked. Once you learn it, you can adapt almost every pasta recipe you cook to ensure it's as perfect as eating out.

1. Undercook the pasta: *Subtract 1 minute from however long the box says to cook the pasta to al dente and set your timer to that number.*

2. Save some pasta water: *Before draining the undercooked pasta, carefully scoop a large measuring cup into the boiling water and reserve some of the cooking water. This water is filled with starch from cooking the pasta and will help tie everything together.*

3. Finish the pasta in the sauce: *Add both the undercooked pasta and some starchy pasta water to the skillet of sauce you've prepared. Bring everything to a simmer and toss constantly for a minute or two (add another splash or two of pasta water, as needed, if things start to dry out too quickly). The starchy water will mix with the sauce to help thicken it and coat the pasta and the pasta will finish cooking during this process.*

CHAPTER 5

Colorful Pastas

Although pasta has a reputation for being less than whole-some, I'd argue that's hardly the case. Sure, it can some-times be made decadent with cream, butter, and such, but it also can be light enough to make it into your weekly dinner routine. When you use pasta as a base for lots of colorful vegetables, it's suddenly something you can feel good about eating. The approach is simple: Flip the proportions so you're eating a vegetable dish with pasta rather than a pasta dish with vegetables. (All that means is you're using less pasta and bumping up the vegetables.) Don't worry! There will still be cheese and other good things tucked inside. Your pasta isn't going to be any less comforting than usual—it's just going to be a whole lot more interesting.

Bucatini Aglio e Olio with Wilted Arugula

Kosher salt

12 ounces (340 g) bucatini, or spaghetti

4 tablespoons (60 ml) extra-virgin olive oil, divided

6 garlic cloves, thinly sliced

½ teaspoon red pepper flakes

5 ounces (about 5 packed cups; 142 g) arugula

Freshly grated Pecorino Romano cheese, for serving

—

Serves 4

Aglio e olio is a pasta dish that finds its origins in the south of Italy—some say Naples, some say the region of Abruzzo. No matter where it comes from, it's a true celebration of Italian pantry cooking. Take lots of aglio (garlic), combine it with good olio (olive oil), plus a healthy dose of fiery red pepper flakes, and you have a pasta sauce that is so much greater than the sum of its parts. Although spaghetti is traditional, I love using toothsome bucatini, which is a bit thicker thanks to a hole running through each strand. One unique thing about this recipe is that instead of serving it with a salad, the salad is tossed right in. A few generous handfuls of peppery arugula wilt quickly when tossed with the hot pasta and you'll find they brighten each bite.

Bring a large pot of salted water to a boil over high heat. Add the pasta and cook for 1 minute less than the package instructions for al dente, about 8 minutes. Reserve 2 cups (480 ml) of pasta water with a measuring cup, then drain the pasta and set it aside.

Meanwhile, heat 3 tablespoons (45 ml) of olive oil in a large, high-sided sauté pan or skillet over medium-low heat. Add the garlic and red pepper flakes and sauté until fragrant and the garlic has softened and is only just beginning to turn light golden (you don't want it to brown), about 5 minutes. Remove from the heat.

Add the reserved pasta water to the pan and bring the mixture to a simmer. Simmer for about 5 minutes until the liquid is reduced by half. Add the bucatini. Toss and stir until the pasta is al dente, and the sauce thickens and coats the pasta, 1 to 2 minutes.

Remove from the heat and add the arugula and remaining 1 tablespoon (15 ml) of olive oil. Toss lightly until the arugula is just wilted, about 1 minute. Serve garnished with grated Pecorino.

No-Cook Summer Tomato Pasta

1 garlic clove, halved

1½ pounds (680 g) plum tomatoes, or Roma tomatoes

¼ cup (10 g) loosely packed chopped fresh basil leaves

1 tablespoon (15 ml) extra-virgin olive oil

½ teaspoon kosher salt

Freshly ground black pepper

12 ounces (340 g) orecchiette, or other short pasta

2 ounces (55 g) ricotta salata cheese

—

Serves 4

When I was living and working on a farm in Tuscany the summer after I graduated college, my teacher, like so many Italians, loved to talk about food. One afternoon, instead of following her usual lesson plan, she held an impromptu cooking class. I can't remember everything we made, but I'll never forget this pasta. She ingeniously rubbed raw cloves of garlic on the inside of a large bowl—a technique that hails from the Southern region of Puglia, where she was from—then dumped hot pasta into it, along with lots of fresh tomatoes and basil. The ingredients took hold of the garlic juices on the bowl to create a bright pasta dish that had just the right amount of seasoning. Rather than the piercing bite of raw garlic, the garlic was mellow and beautifully blended.

—

Make this in late summer, when tomatoes are at their absolute sweetest and juiciest. Grating them on a box grater results in a loose, chunky sauce for the orecchiette cups to hold (though other short pasta shapes, such as gemelli and fusilli, work great, too). Oh, and don't bother washing the grater right away. You'll use it to grate salty ricotta salata cheese over the top of each bowl, which adds a bit of a sharp kick to every bite.

Rub the garlic clove halves vigorously all over the inside of a large bowl.

Set a box grater over the garlic-rubbed bowl and use the side with the large holes to grate the tomatoes into the bowl. Discard the flattened skin and stem left behind. Gently stir in the basil, olive oil, salt, and several grinds of black pepper; mix well. Let the mixture marinate while you cook the pasta.

Bring a large pot of salted water to a boil over high heat. Add the pasta and cook according to the package instructions until al dente, about 9 minutes. Drain the pasta, then transfer it to the bowl of tomatoes. Toss well to combine.

Using the large holes of the box grater, grate ricotta salata over the pasta before serving.

Note:

You'll likely have a nub of garlic leftover after rubbing the bowl. Rather than toss it, use it to make Everyday Vinaigrette (page 27) for a dinner side salad or wrap it up and tuck it in the fridge for another use.

Orzo Skillet with Shrimp and Feta

1 (28-ounce, or 794 g) can whole peeled tomatoes

1 tablespoon (15 ml) extra-virgin olive oil

1½ cups (10 ounces, or 280 g) orzo

4 garlic cloves, minced

½ teaspoon dried oregano

¼ teaspoon red pepper flakes

Kosher salt

12 ounces (340 g) uncooked medium peeled and deveined shrimp

Freshly ground black pepper

3 ounces (85 g) feta cheese, crumbled (about ¾ cup)

Coarsely chopped fresh mint, for serving

—

Serves 4

There are a whole lot of culinary faux pas out there—combining seafood and cheese is one of them. I can't say you'll find me grating Parmesan cheese over my linguine and clams anytime soon—but just like everything, there are exceptions. This dish is one of them. It's inspired by garides saganaki, *a classic Greek dish of shrimp swimming in spiced tomato sauce that's topped with crumbled feta and broiled. Both the shrimp and feta are inherently briny, so it's a pretty natural match, and the salty cheese plays so well off the sweet crustaceans. Here I couldn't help but add chewy, rice-like orzo, which cooks right in the tomato sauce so there's no need to boil a separate pot of water. It's a one-pan dinner that may feel like you're breaking some rules, but you'll be happy you did.*

Empty the canned tomatoes with their juices into a large bowl and carefully crush them with your hands (you'll have some bite-size pieces remaining). Set aside.

Place a rack in the top third of the oven (6 to 8 inches, or 15 to 20 cm, from the broiling element) and preheat the broiler to high.

Heat the olive oil in a large cast iron or other oven-safe skillet over medium. Add the orzo and cook, stirring occasionally, until fragrant and lightly toasted, 2 to 3 minutes. Add the garlic and sauté until fragrant, about 1 minute. Add the crushed tomatoes, oregano, red pepper flakes, and ½ teaspoon of salt. Stir to combine and bring to a boil. Reduce to a simmer and cook, uncovered, until the pasta is al dente, the liquid is absorbed, and a thick sauce has formed, about 10 minutes. Stir a few times while simmering to ensure the orzo doesn't stick to the bottom of the skillet.

Meanwhile, pat the shrimp dry with paper towels and season all over with salt and pepper.

Stir the orzo once more, spread it into an even layer, and scatter the shrimp and feta over the top. Transfer the skillet to the oven and broil until the shrimp are pink and opaque and the feta is softened and lightly browned, 3 to 4 minutes. Garnish with mint before serving.

Caramelized Mushroom Pasta with Crispy Prosciutto

Kosher salt

4 thin prosciutto slices

2 tablespoons (30 ml) extra-virgin olive oil, divided

1 pound (454 g) cremini mushrooms, quartered

12 ounces (340 g) campanelle, or other short pasta

Freshly ground black pepper

4 garlic cloves, minced

1 tablespoon (3 g) fresh thyme leaves

¼ cup (60 ml) dry white wine

Freshly shaved Parmesan cheese, for serving

—

Serves 4

Mushrooms are one of my favorite ingredients to toss into a pasta dish because of how much meatiness they add. By opting for bite-size quarters instead of thin slices, they're easier to grab with a forkful of pasta and they match the pasta's al dente-ness. Although sautéing them is well and good, here I up both their flavor and texture by caramelizing them. To caramelize the mushrooms, sear them in batches to give them the space needed to develop a deep, golden brown crust, which really helps draw out their umami-rich flavor. Add plenty of garlic and thyme to the mix, along with crispy shards of prosciutto for good measure and the result is a savory, earthy pasta that's easy to love.

Bring a large pot of salted water to a boil over high heat.

Heat a large, high-sided sauté pan or skillet over medium heat. Add 2 prosciutto slices to the pan, in a single layer, and cook until they curl and are lightly browned underneath, 2 to 3 minutes. Flip the prosciutto and let cook until browned on the other side, 2 to 3 minutes more. Transfer the prosciutto to a paper towel–lined plate and repeat with the remaining 2 slices.

Pour 1 tablespoon (15 ml) of olive oil into the pan. Add half the mushrooms in a single layer (try to get as many cut-side down as you can, but don't stress too much about it), and cook undisturbed until browned well on the bottom but not fully cooked, 3 to 5 minutes. Transfer to a plate. Add the remaining 1 tablespoon (15 ml) of olive oil to the pan and repeat with the remaining mushrooms.

Continues >

Continued

Meanwhile, add the pasta to the boiling water and cook for 1 minute less than the package instructions for al dente, about 9 minutes.

Once the second batch of mushrooms is browned well on the bottom, return the rest of the mushrooms to the pan and add the garlic and thyme. Season with salt and pepper and cook, stirring once or twice, until the mushrooms are fragrant and just tender, about 2 minutes more. Pour the wine into the pan and simmer, using a wooden spoon to scrape up the browned bits that have formed on the bottom of the pan, until some but not all of the liquid has evaporated, 1 minute or less; remove from the heat.

When the pasta is ready, reserve ½ cup (120 ml) of pasta water with a measuring cup, then drain the pasta. Add the pasta and reserved pasta water to the pan and bring to a simmer. Cook, tossing and stirring, until the pasta is al dente and the sauce thickens and coats the pasta, 1 to 2 minutes. Remove from the heat.

Break the prosciutto into small pieces and stir half into the pasta. Serve garnished with the remaining prosciutto and shaved Parmesan.

Note:

Cooking the mushrooms in two batches may seem fussy but it's for good reason—they need space to caramelize. Crowd all the mushrooms in the pan and the liquid they naturally release won't have enough room to evaporate, causing the mushrooms to steam rather than brown.

Lemony Yogurt and Zucchini Linguine

2 (about 1 pound, or 454 g, total) zucchini, ends trimmed

1 teaspoon kosher salt, plus more for the cooking water

12 ounces (340 g) linguine

2 tablespoons (30 ml) extra-virgin olive oil

3 garlic cloves, minced

¾ cup (170 g) whole milk plain Greek yogurt

¼ cup (14 g) packed fresh finely grated Pecorino Romano cheese, plus more for serving

Finely grated zest of 1 lemon

Juice of 1 lemon

Freshly ground black pepper

2 tablespoons (6 g) chopped fresh mint

¼ cup (10 g) loosely packed chopped fresh basil leaves, divided

———

Serves 4

When zucchini noodles, a.k.a. zoodles, came along several years ago, you just couldn't persuade me. I still feel this way, even after trying them once or twice, so to be clear: This is not a zoodle recipe. What it is, instead, is a pasta recipe with lots of grated zucchini, so the two ingredients live in harmony rather than the latter trying to pose as an imposter. Oh, plus, zucchini linguine is just fun to say.

———

The true star here, though, is the yogurt. Greek yogurt isn't the most common ingredient in a pasta dish, but perhaps it should be. Toss a few big dollops into the mix and it melts almost instantly into a creamy sauce that delivers just the right amount of tang to keep each twirl from feeling weighed down.

Shred the zucchini using the shredding blade of a food processor or the large holes of a box grater on an angle to achieve long shreds. Transfer to a fine-mesh strainer set over a bowl. Toss with the salt and set aside for 10 minutes.

Using your hands or a wooden spoon, press down on the zucchini to push out some of its liquid. Then wrap it in a clean kitchen towel and squeeze out as much water as you can to get it as dry as possible. Set aside.

Bring a large pot of salted water to a boil over high heat. Add the linguine and cook according to the package instructions until al dente, about 10 minutes.

Meanwhile, heat the olive oil in a large, high-sided sauté pan or skillet over medium-low heat. Add the garlic and sauté until fragrant and just beginning to turn light golden brown, 3 to 5 minutes. Remove from the heat.

When the pasta is ready, reserve 1 cup (240 ml) of pasta water with a measuring cup, then drain the pasta. With the pan still off the heat, add the pasta, reserved zucchini, yogurt, Pecorino, lemon zest and juice, and several grinds of black pepper. Toss, adding a spoonful of reserved pasta water at a time, as needed, until the yogurt loosens a bit and coats the pasta and zucchini in a creamy sauce (you most likely will not use all the pasta water).

Add the mint and half the basil and toss again to combine. Serve garnished with the remaining basil and additional grated Pecorino.

Spaghetti and Meatball Ragù

1 (28-ounce, or 794 g) can whole peeled tomatoes

1 pound (454 g) ground meat (beef, pork, turkey, or a combination)

⅔ cup (36 g) Freezer Bread Crumbs (page 23), or panko bread crumbs

¼ cup (60 ml) whole milk

¼ cup (14 g) packed fresh finely grated Parmesan cheese, plus more for serving

¼ cup (10 g) loosely packed chopped fresh parsley

1 large egg

3 garlic cloves, minced, divided

Kosher salt

Freshly ground black pepper

2 tablespoons (30 ml) extra-virgin olive oil

1 small yellow onion, finely chopped

¼ teaspoon red pepper flakes (optional)

1 pound (454 g) spaghetti

—

Serves 6

Spaghetti and meatballs is hardly true Mediterranean fare, but my devout Italian-American husband deeply loves it. I, on the other hand, have long been frustrated by the dish—it's most definitely proof of my Type-A personality. When the meatballs are plopped down on the spaghetti, they weigh the strands down, so you have to maneuver them to the side, cut them, then try to incorporate a bite of meatball into each twirl of pasta. The mechanics just never felt right to me, which is why my preference is to enjoy them separately. Yet, as Joe grew up eating it, it's pure comfort food to him, so he craves the combo frequently. That's how this recipe came about—I made it in an attempt to meet halfway. Crumbling the meatballs into the sauce creates a quick ragu that makes for much easier eating but doesn't completely compromise the major components of the dish, so now we're both happy.

—

Oh, and I know this pasta is a bit of an outlier in the colorful scheme I've set forth but that's okay because I'd honestly be remiss not to include it. Serve it with The Easiest Arugula Salad (page 72), and you've just made the whole table colorful.

Place a rack in the middle of the oven and preheat the oven to 400°F (200°C). Line a rimmed sheet pan with parchment paper. Set aside.

Empty the canned tomatoes with their juices into a large bowl and carefully crush them with hands (you'll have some bite-size pieces remaining). Set aside.

Place the ground meat, bread crumbs, milk, Parmesan, parsley, egg, half the garlic, 1 teaspoon of salt, and several grinds of black pepper into a large bowl. Combine lightly with a fork then use your hands to form the mixture into 2-inch (5 cm) meatballs (14 to 16 meatballs) and place them on the prepared pan.

Continues >

Bake the meatballs until browned and an instant-read thermometer inserted into the middle reads 165°F (74°C), 15 to 20 minutes. Remove from the oven and set aside until cool enough to handle, about 10 minutes.

Meanwhile, heat the olive oil in a medium saucepan over medium heat. Add the onion and sauté until softened and translucent, about 5 minutes. Add remaining garlic and sauté until fragrant, about 1 minute. Carefully pour the crushed tomatoes into the pan, then stir in the red pepper flakes (if using) and a generous pinch of salt. Bring the sauce to a simmer.

Crumble the meatballs into about 1-inch (2.5 cm) chunks and stir them into the sauce. Continue to gently simmer, stirring occasionally, while you cook the pasta. Taste and season with additional salt, as needed.

Bring a large pot of salted water to a boil over high heat. Add the spaghetti and cook according to the package instructions until al dente, about 10 minutes. Drain the pasta, return it to the pot off the heat, and ladle in the meatball ragù. Toss to combine and serve garnished with plenty of grated Parmesan.

Notes:

This recipe is pretty flexible—use any combination of ground meat you prefer for the meatballs. I usually alternate between ground turkey or a 50/50 mix of ground beef and pork.

The tomato sauce comes together quickly here, but if you're just not in the mood to bother (which is totally okay!), don't hesitate to swap in a jar of good quality marinara, such as Rao's. Just bring the sauce to a simmer in a large pot and crumble the meatballs right into it.

Balsamic Brown Butter Tortellini with Spinach and Hazelnuts

Kosher salt

6 tablespoons (84 g) unsalted butter

½ cup (70 g) hazelnuts, chopped

2 tablespoons (20 g) finely chopped shallot

4 tablespoons (60 ml) balsamic vinegar, divided

Freshly ground black pepper

2 (9- or 10-ounce, or 255 or 283 g) packages fresh or frozen cheese tortellini, or 1 (16- to 20-ounce, or 454 to 567 g) bag fresh or frozen cheese tortellini

5 ounces (about 5 packed cups; 142 g) baby spinach

Freshly shaved Parmesan cheese, for serving

———

Serves 4 to 6

Cooking something that feels fancy doesn't necessarily mean toiling for hours in the kitchen. If you don't believe me, take this recipe as proof. Fresh or frozen cheese tortellini is ubiquitous in grocery stores and more than fine when tossed with marinara sauce for a quick meal. But, in just as little time, it can become a dinner that deserves an impromptu bottle of wine after a harried Wednesday. The secret is a super-easy-to-make brown butter sauce, which makes pretty much anyone weak in the knees. The situation would be well and good if left at that but to make it feel extra special, a surprise ingredient doesn't hurt. In this case, it's hazelnuts. They amp up the toasted flavor of the brown butter and add just enough crunch to keep each bite interesting.

Bring a large pot of salted water to a boil over high heat.

Meanwhile, cut the butter into a few pieces and place it in a large, high-sided sauté pan or skillet over medium heat to melt. Cook, stirring occasionally, until the butter is pale golden, about 3 minutes. Add the hazelnuts and cook, stirring occasionally, until the nuts are glossy and golden and the butter is just beginning to turn toasted brown and have a nutty aroma, 2 to 3 minutes. Add the shallot and sauté until softened, about 1 minute more. Remove from the heat and carefully stir in 3 tablespoons (45 ml) of vinegar, ¼ teaspoon of salt, and several grinds of black pepper.

Add the tortellini to the boiling water and cook for 1 minute less than the package instructions for al dente.

Continues >

Continued

When the tortellini are ready, reserve ¼ cup (60 ml) of pasta water with a measuring cup, then drain the tortellini. Add the reserved pasta water and tortellini to the pan and bring the mixture to a simmer. Add the spinach, handful by handful, tossing and gently stirring until the spinach has wilted and the sauce has thickened enough to coat the pasta evenly, 1 to 2 minutes.

Remove from the heat and stir in the remaining 1 tablespoon (15 ml) of vinegar. Taste and season with additional salt and pepper, as needed. Serve garnished with shaved Parmesan.

How to Brown Butter

Though there's hardly anything wrong with butter as-is, allowing it to transform into something so fragrant and nutty that it's arguably richer than its original state is pure kitchen magic. The technique is fairly easy to master but it does require a close eye, as burned butter isn't quite as enchanting.

When possible, reach for a light-colored pan so you can easily see the butter browning and know when it's done. Start with unsalted butter (it can be cold, straight from the fridge), in any amount, but if it's more than a couple tablespoons, cut it into equal-size pieces to ensure even melting and browning. Place the butter in the pan and turn the heat to medium. Let the butter melt, stirring occasionally, until it begins to foam. Continue cooking and stirring occasionally. The foam will subside, the color will start to change, and lightly browned specks will begin to form at the bottom of the pan. The overall color of the butter will transform from yellow to golden tan to deep toasted brown and the butter will have a nutty, caramelized aroma. Once it reaches this stage, immediately remove it from the heat to prevent it from browning any further and burning.

Pasta with Burst Cherry Tomatoes and Swordfish

1 pound (454 g) swordfish

Kosher salt

Freshly ground black pepper

2 tablespoons (30 ml) extra-virgin olive oil

2 pints (about 4 cups, or 600 g) cherry tomatoes, or grape tomatoes

12 ounces (340 g) casarecce, or other short pasta

4 garlic cloves, thinly sliced

½ teaspoon red pepper flakes

¼ cup (60 ml) dry white wine

¼ cup (10 g) loosely packed chopped fresh parsley

—

Serves 4

The minute I tasted a dish similar to this one on the coast of Sicily, I knew I had to recreate it. Swordfish is a common ingredient in pasta there and adds such great meaty texture without weighing things down. As the tomatoes burst, they form a chunky sauce that pairs perfectly with bite-size pieces of fish. Casarecce is a short, twisted pasta that's Sicilian in origin and becoming easier to find at major grocery stores these days, but feel free to use any short shape you like.

Trim the skin from the swordfish and cut the flesh into bite-size cubes, ½ to ¾ inch (1 to 2 cm) in size. Season all over with salt and pepper and set aside. Bring a large pot of salted water to a boil over high heat.

Heat the olive oil in a large, high-sided sauté pan or skillet over medium heat. Add the tomatoes and a generous pinch of salt. Cook, stirring occasionally, until the tomatoes start to burst and release some of their juices, 8 to 10 minutes. Add the garlic and red pepper flakes and sauté until fragrant, about 1 minute. Push the tomato mixture to one side of the skillet.

Meanwhile, add the pasta to the boiling water and cook for 1 minute less than the package instructions for al dente, about 8 minutes.

Spread the swordfish in a single layer in the open space of the sauté pan. Cook until lightly browned on the bottom, about 1 minute. Flip the fish cubes and continue to cook on the other side until just cooked through, 2 to 3 minutes more. Stir to combine the fish with the tomatoes.

Pour the wine into the pan and simmer, using a wooden spoon to scrape up any browned bits that may have formed on the bottom on the pan, until some but not all of the liquid has evaporated, 1 minute or less. Remove from the heat.

When the pasta is ready, reserve ½ cup (120 ml) of pasta water with a measuring cup, then drain the pasta. Add the pasta and reserved pasta water to the pan and bring the mixture to a simmer. Cook, tossing and stirring, until the pasta is al dente and the sauce thickens and coats the pasta, 1 to 2 minutes. Remove from the heat. Add the parsley, toss to combine, and serve.

Pesto Pasta with Charred Radicchio

Kosher salt

12 ounces (340 g) rigatoni, or other short tubular pasta

1 medium or 2 small heads (about 12 ounces, or 340 g) radicchio, cored, quartered, and cut crosswise into 1-inch (2.5 cm)-wide strips (about 6 cups)

1 tablespoon (15 ml) extra-virgin olive oil

Freshly ground black pepper

1 batch Any Herb Pesto (page 20), or ¾ cup (180 g) good quality store-bought pesto

Freshly grated Parmesan cheese, for serving

—

Serves 4

I'll be the first to admit: Pasta tossed with nothing but good pesto sauce doesn't need much tinkering. However, I will say radicchio does something extra magical to it. Although the vegetable's inherent bitterness can be jarring to those unaccustomed, it's tamed when thrown under the broiler for a few minutes until the edges soften and char. To be sure, it still holds some of its bite, which is a good thing, because it offsets the richness of the oil and cheese-heavy sauce—not to mention its crimson hue adds a striking pop of color to the emerald green bowl.

Place a rack in the top third of the oven (6 to 8 inches, or 15 to 20 cm, from the broiling element) and preheat to broil.

Bring a large pot of salted water to a boil over high heat. Add the pasta and cook according to the package instructions until al dente, about 12 minutes.

Place the radicchio on a rimmed sheet pan. Drizzle with the olive oil, season with salt and pepper, and toss to coat. Spread into a single layer and broil until the radicchio just begins to wilt and the edges are lightly charred, 2 to 3 minutes.

Reserve ¼ cup (60 ml) of pasta water with a measuring cup, then drain the pasta. Return the pasta to the pot, off the heat.

Add the pesto to the pasta and toss to combine. If needed, add the reserved pasta water, a spoonful at a time, to loosen the sauce so the pasta is evenly coated. (You may not have to use it at all and, if you do, you'll likely not use all of it.) Add the radicchio, toss again, and serve, garnished with grated Parmesan.

Melted Broccoli Pasta with Capers and Anchovies

Kosher salt

2 heads (about 1 pound, or 454 g, total) broccoli, cut into bite-size florets

12 ounces (340 g) whole-wheat penne pasta, or other short tubular pasta

3 tablespoons (45 ml) extra-virgin olive oil, divided

1 cup (54 g) Freezer Bread Crumbs (page 23), or panko bread crumbs

4 oil-packed anchovy fillets

¼ cup (36 g) capers, chopped if large (rinsed well if salt-packed)

2 garlic cloves, minced

¼ teaspoon red pepper flakes

—

Serves 4

When whole-wheat pasta first hit grocery store shelves years ago, it seemed like it was all or nothing. Either wipe your pantry clean of regular pasta in favor of this so-called better choice or just stop eating pasta altogether. Despite all its nutritional benefits, most of us (myself included) just couldn't get past the cardboard-like texture and flavor—pasta seemed like it might forever be doomed.

—

Luckily, we've recovered from those dark years, thanks to better-tasting whole-wheat pasta and the realization that regular pasta is irreplaceable. The truth is, there's a time and a place for whole-wheat pasta. Its nutty, earthy flavor isn't the best match with a light tomato sauce, but it works quite well with bolder ingredients like capers and anchovies, which can stand up to the pasta's wholesomeness. Hearty vegetables pair well, too. Here, broccoli is cooked down and transformed into an extra-chunky, extra-savory sauce. For even more texture, grated cheese is swapped for toasted bread crumbs. In Italy, they're known as pangrattato, *or "grated bread," as peasants once used them as a cheese replacement on their pasta because they couldn't afford the real deal. Nowadays both are easily within reach, but the crunch they add here makes it easy to leave the Parmesan behind.*

Bring a large pot of salted water to a boil over high heat. Add the broccoli florets and cook until bright green and crisp-tender, 2 to 3 minutes. Using a slotted spoon, transfer the broccoli to a large bowl.

Add the pasta to the boiling water and cook for 1 minute less than the package instructions for al dente, about 9 minutes.

Continues >

Continued

Meanwhile, toast the bread crumbs. Heat 1 tablespoon (15 ml) of olive oil in a large, high-sided sauté pan or skillet over medium heat. Add the bread crumbs and sauté until the crumbs are golden brown and crisp, 4 to 5 minutes. Transfer to a small bowl and set aside.

Pour the remaining 2 tablespoons (30 ml) of olive oil into the pan. Add the anchovies and sauté until they disintegrate, about 1 minute. Add the capers, garlic, and red pepper flakes. Sauté until fragrant, about 1 minute, and remove from the heat.

When the pasta is ready, reserve 1½ cups (360 ml) of pasta water with a measuring cup, then drain the pasta. Add the broccoli and reserved pasta water to the pan and bring to a simmer. Continue to simmer, using a wooden spoon to break the florets into small pieces as they become more tender, until the water is reduced by about half and you've been able to break apart enough florets that you're left with a very chunky mixture, 5 to 7 minutes.

Add the pasta to the pan. Cook, tossing and stirring, until the pasta is al dente and the sauce thickens and coats the pasta, 1 to 2 minutes. Remove from the heat, add half the toasted bread crumbs, and toss again to combine. Serve garnished with the remaining toasted bread crumbs.

Note:

You can also make this pasta with cauliflower instead of broccoli. It will be a bit less colorful but equally as flavorful and feel-good.

Israeli Couscous Salad with Herbs, Green Olives, and Pistachios

4 tablespoons (60 ml) extra-virgin olive oil, divided

2 tablespoons (20 g) finely chopped shallot

2 tablespoons (30 ml) red wine vinegar

Kosher salt

Freshly ground black pepper

1½ cups (225 g) whole-wheat or regular Israeli (pearl) couscous

3 cups (710 ml) water

⅓ cup (55 g) shelled, raw pistachios

1½ cups (about 9 ounces, or 255 g) Castelvetrano olives, or another mild green olive such as Cerignola, pitted and coarsely chopped

½ cup (20 g) loosely packed chopped fresh cilantro

½ cup (20 g) loosely packed chopped fresh parsley

¼ cup (10 g) loosely packed chopped fresh dill

———

Serves 4 to 6

Israeli couscous is one of my favorite ingredients to play around with. It also goes by the name pearl couscous, which is especially fitting due to its pearl-like shape and size. It's made from semolina flour, the same flour used to make dried pasta, so it, too, is a type of pasta and has a wonderfully chewy texture. Though you can find it made with both white and whole-wheat flours, I especially like the latter here for its nutty flavor that's a welcomed contrast to buttery green olives (not to mention an added boost of fiber and nutrients). It's not always easy to find, though, so don't sweat it if you can only get your hands on regular Israeli couscous. Enjoy this salad for lunch or dinner, either as a side dish or the main affair. Serve it as is, of course, or try it over greens, with chickpeas stirred in, or even topped with shrimp, salmon, or a fried egg.

Place a rack in the middle of the oven and preheat the oven to 350°F (180°C).

In a large bowl, whisk 3 tablespoons (454 ml) of olive oil, the shallot, vinegar, a generous pinch of salt, and several grinds of black pepper until combined and emulsified. Set aside.

Heat the remaining 1 tablespoon (15 ml) of olive oil in a medium saucepan over medium heat. Add the couscous and cook, stirring occasionally, until toasted and light golden brown, about 3 minutes. Add the water and ½ teaspoon of salt, stir to combine, and bring to a boil. Reduce the heat and simmer, uncovered, until the couscous is tender, about 10 minutes. Drain the couscous through a fine-mesh strainer to remove any excess cooking liquid.

Continues >

Continued

Transfer the hot couscous to the bowl of dressing and stir to combine. Let sit, stirring occasionally, to cool and let the flavors combine, 10 to 15 minutes.

Meanwhile, toast the pistachios. Spread the pistachios on a rimmed sheet pan and bake, stirring halfway through, until golden brown, about 5 minutes. Let cool for 5 minutes, then coarsely chop.

Stir the olives, herbs, and pistachios into the couscous. Taste and season with additional salt and pepper, as needed. Serve warm or at room temperature.

The Art of the Make-Ahead Pasta Salad

Pasta salads are one my favorite things to make for potlucks, picnics, and even weekday lunches because of their ability to be made ahead and kept well in the fridge for days. However, there are a couple of keys to success. Although it doesn't matter as much if you're simply packing up the salad for your own lunch, if you're bringing it to a gathering, hold off on stirring in the herbs until just before serving. This ensures they stay bright green and maintain their fresh bite. Also, let the salad come fully to room temperature—a cold pasta salad delivers muted flavors. And finally, give it a taste before digging in. The pasta absorbs a whole lot of the vinaigrette when stored so I always find it needs another glug or two of olive oil and vinegar, and maybe another pinch of salt and pepper, to bring it fully back to life.

Baked Spinach Artichoke Gnudi

2 tablespoons (30 ml) extra-virgin olive oil

2 cups (15 or 16 ounces, or 425 to 454 g) high-quality whole milk ricotta

1 (16-ounce, or 454 g) bag frozen chopped spinach, thawed and squeezed dry

¾ cup (42 g) packed fresh finely grated Parmesan cheese, divided

1 large egg

½ teaspoon kosher salt

Freshly ground black pepper

¼ cup (32 g) all-purpose flour

1 (12-ounce, or 340 g) jar marinated artichokes, drained well and coarsely chopped

2 garlic cloves, thinly sliced

½ lemon

—

Serves 4

In Tuscan slang, gnudi *means "naked" and it's actually just that: The naked spinach and ricotta filling of ravioli without the pasta clothing it. They're quite similar to ricotta gnocchi: tender and pillow-y. Although the delicate dumplings are traditionally boiled, I've found that baking them alleviates any risk of their falling apart. Here, I couldn't help but bake them on a bed of marinated artichokes for a playful twist on the classic dip that, though truly all-American, has flavors rooted in the Mediterranean.*

Place a rack in the top third of the oven (6 to 8 inches, or 15 to 20 cm, from the broiling element) and preheat the oven to 425°F (220°C). Pour 2 tablespoons (30 ml) of olive oil in a 9 × 13-inch (23 × 33 cm) or other 3-quart (3 L) baking dish. Tilt the dish to coat it evenly. Set aside.

In a large bowl, combine the ricotta, spinach, ½ cup (28 g) of Parmesan, the egg, salt, and several grinds of black pepper. Add the flour and stir to just combine.

Spread the artichokes into an even layer in the prepared baking dish and sprinkle with garlic. Use a size 40 (1½-tablespoon) cookie scoop or 2 spoons to drop golf ball–size gnudi on top of the artichokes, spacing them about ½ inch (1 cm) apart.

Bake until the tops of the gnudi are firm and the artichokes are lightly browned, about 30 minutes. Remove the baking dish from the oven and turn on the broiler. Sprinkle the remaining ¼ cup (14 g) of Parmesan evenly over the top of the gnudi and artichokes, return the baking dish to the oven, and broil until the gnudi are lightly browned, 2 to 3 minutes. Let cool for 5 minutes. Squeeze the lemon half over the gnudi and artichokes and serve.

CHAPTER 6

Gathering Dishes

A gathering doesn't necessarily mean the kind with lots
of people involved. A small crowd should never feel like
any less of an occasion to share a good meal. What I cook
midweek or on a quiet Sunday night isn't always a whole lot
different from what I cook when friends come by for dinner
on Saturday night. Of course, there are hectic Wednesdays
when some semblance of a civilized dinner seems impossible, but if you're able to feed yourself well as many nights a
week as possible, I deem that a major win. To do that, make
simple the goal and lean on good ingredients. Unfussy main
dishes have a magical way of coming together easily enough
that whatever the situation may be or however many
mouths you're feeding, what you're gathering around the
table for always feels special.

Thyme Pesto Roast Chicken with Crispy Potatoes

1½ pounds (680 g) small red-skinned potatoes, halved

1 tablespoon (15 ml) extra-virgin olive oil

Kosher salt

Freshly ground black pepper

1 batch parsley and thyme variation Any Herb Pesto (page 20), divided

1 lemon, halved crosswise

1 (3½- to 4- pound, or 1.6 to 1.8 kg) whole chicken, at room temperature

—

Serves 4

Note:

Getting the pesto under the skin is a bit of a messy process. The skin might break a little, but don't worry too much. Spread the pesto underneath the best you can, then slather any bits leftover in the bowl or on your hand over the outside of the bird.

Thyme is a perfect match for chicken. Turning it into pesto gives you an olive oil–rich sauce that, when rubbed under the skin, helps prevent the meat from drying out as it roasts. Although you can roast the bird on its own, tossing a bunch of potatoes into the pan means you almost have a complete dinner on your hands. (It also means those potatoes soak up a lot of the chicken's flavorful juices.) I typically serve this with a simple salad, but in summer, a platter of thick, juicy tomato slices alongside instead just can't be beat.

Place a rack in the middle of the oven and preheat the oven to 450°F (230°C).

Place the potatoes in a large baking dish, roasting pan, or cast iron skillet. Drizzle with the olive oil, season with salt and pepper, and toss to coat.

Place ¼ cup (60 g) of pesto in a small bowl (reserve the remaining ½ cup [120 g] of pesto for seasoning the chicken). Squeeze the juice of both lemon halves into the small bowl (reserve the squeezed halves) and stir to combine. Set aside.

Pat the chicken dry with a paper towel. Using your fingers, gently loosen and pull away the skin from the breasts, legs, and back. Stuff the reserved ½ cup (120 g) of pesto under the skin, little by little, spreading it against the meat all over the breasts, legs, and back.

Generously season the chicken on all sides, inside and out, with salt and pepper. Place the chicken, breast-side up, on top of the potatoes. Stuff both reserved squeezed lemon halves into the chicken's cavity.

Transfer the baking dish to the oven and immediately lower the oven temperature to 400°F (200°C). Roast until an instant-read thermometer inserted into the thickest part of the chicken's thigh reads 170°F (77°C), the wings and legs feel loose when you wiggle them gently, and the juices run clear, 1 to 1½ hours.

Transfer the chicken to a cutting board. Give the potatoes a toss and return them to the oven to continue to roast and crisp while you let the chicken rest for 10 minutes and then carve it.

After carving the chicken, remove the potatoes from the oven and transfer them to a serving dish. Stir some of the pan juices that remain in the baking dish or skillet into the reserved lemon pesto sauce to thin it just enough so it's easy to drizzle. Serve the chicken and potatoes with the reserved lemon pesto sauce on the side to be spooned over both as desired.

Salmon in Crazy Water

I first learned about acqua pazza, *or "crazy water," from the late, great chef and cookbook author Marcella Hazan. The tomato-based broth that's used as a poaching liquid, typically for flaky white fish, is traditional in the southern Italian region of Campania. I was initially drawn in by the silly name but quickly fell for the easily adaptable broth. It's simply simmered tomatoes and water, which means it can be flavored with as few or as many aromatics and herbs as you'd like. Here, I beef up the broth with onion and fennel seeds, so it can hold up to meaty salmon fillets. It's a meal that's light yet satisfying and begs to be served with bread to mop up the savory broth.*

2 tablespoons (30 ml) extra-virgin olive oil

3 garlic cloves, thinly sliced

½ teaspoon fennel seeds

¼ teaspoon red pepper flakes

1½ pounds (680 g) plum tomatoes, or Roma tomatoes, coarsely chopped into 1-inch (2.5 cm) pieces

1 small yellow onion, halved and thinly sliced

Kosher salt

1 cup (240 ml) water

½ cup (120 ml) dry white wine

1½ pounds (680 g) salmon fillet, skinned and cut into 4 (6-ounce, or 170 g) pieces

Coarsely chopped fresh parsley, for serving

Good bread, for serving (optional)

—

Serves 4

Heat the olive oil in a large, high-side sauté pan or skillet over medium heat. Add the garlic, fennel seeds, and red pepper flakes and sauté until fragrant, about 1 minute. Add the tomatoes, onion, and ½ teaspoon of salt and sauté until the tomatoes break down to release their juices and the onion is softened and translucent, about 5 minutes.

Add the water and wine and bring the liquid to a gentle simmer. Simmer, uncovered, until the liquid reduces by about one fourth, 5 to 10 minutes. Taste and season with additional salt, as needed.

Season the salmon with salt and place it in the pan. Reduce the heat to medium-low, cover the pan, and simmer until the fish just begins to flake, 5 to 8 minutes, depending on the thickness of your fillets. An instant-read thermometer inserted into the middle of the thickest fillet should read 120°F to 130°F (49°C to 54.5°C) for medium-rare or 135°F to 145°F (57°C to 63°C) if you prefer your salmon more well done.

Transfer the salmon fillets to 4 shallow bowls and spoon the broth around them. Sprinkle with parsley and serve with bread, if desired.

Caramelized Leek and Fennel Galette with Blue Cheese

For Crust:

1 cup (128 g) whole-wheat flour

¾ cup (96 g) all-purpose flour

½ teaspoon kosher salt

⅓ cup (80 ml) extra-virgin olive oil

⅓ cup (80 ml) water

1 teaspoon red wine vinegar

For Filling and Assembly:

3 tablespoons (45 ml) extra-virgin olive oil

2 medium fennel bulbs, trimmed, quartered, and thinly sliced (reserve a handful of chopped fronds for garnish, if desired)

2 medium leeks, white and light green parts only, cleaned and thinly sliced into half-moons

Kosher salt

Freshly ground black pepper

3 ounces (85 g) blue cheese, crumbled (about ¾ cup), divided

All-purpose flour, for dusting

2 teaspoons Dijon mustard

Serves 4 to 6 as a main, 8 as an appetizer or side dish

Galettes are well worth getting to know, if you haven't already had the pleasure. A galette is a lazy person's pie. Instead of the hassle involved in fitting your crust into a pie pan and painstakingly crimping it, a galette is assembled right on the baking sheet. It hardly needs to look perfect—in fact, the rustic look is actually what you're after. Here, a crust made from whole-wheat flour and olive oil not only makes this savory pie more wholesome, it means you don't have to fuss over cold butter cubes. The filling is deeply flavored and pungent thanks to the caramelized vegetables and blue cheese. A swipe of Dijon between the filling and the crust adds to this fact while also protecting the crust from any excess moisture in the vegetables that might make it soggy. I like to serve this galette in generous slices alongside greens tossed with Everyday Vinaigrette (page 27).

To make the crust: In a large bowl, combine the whole-wheat flour, all-purpose flour, and salt. Add the olive oil and mix with a fork until crumbly. Pour in the water and vinegar. Using a fork or your hands, combine and lightly mix until a dough ball forms. The dough will be a bit wet, but don't worry, the whole-wheat flour will absorb the extra moisture when it rests. Wrap the dough ball tightly in plastic wrap and refrigerate for at least 45 minutes while you make the filling, or up to a day.

To make the filling: Heat the olive oil in a large, high-sided sauté pan or skillet over medium heat. Add the fennel and leeks, season with salt and pepper, and sauté, lowering the heat if any vegetables start to burn, until the vegetables are soft, caramelized, and reduced by half, about 30 minutes. Be sure to scrape up any browned bits that accumulate on the bottom of the pan as you cook the vegetables—that's flavor! Remove the pan from the heat and let the vegetables cool for 10 minutes. Once cool, gently stir in half the blue cheese. Taste and season with additional salt and pepper, as needed.

Continues >

Continued

To assemble the galette: Place a rack in the middle of the oven and preheat the oven to 400°F (200°C). Tear a piece of parchment paper, roughly the size of a baking sheet, and place it on a work surface. Lightly dust the parchment with flour.

Unwrap the dough and place it on prepared parchment paper. Sprinkle the dough with flour and, using a rolling pin, roll it into a round about 12 inches (30 cm) in diameter. Carefully transfer the parchment paper, with the rolled-out dough on it, to a baking sheet.

Spread the Dijon evenly on top of the dough, leaving about a 1½- to 2-inch (3.5 to 5 cm) border. Spoon the vegetable filling on top of the mustard. Gently fold the edges of the dough over the filling, covering about 1½ to 2 inches (3.5 to 5 cm) of the filling and pleating the dough about every 2 inches (5 cm) as you go.

Bake until the crust is firm and lightly golden, 30 to 35 minutes. Sprinkle the filling with the remaining blue cheese and continue to bake until the cheese just melts, 3 to 5 minutes more.

Let the galette cool for at least 5 to 10 minutes before transferring it to a serving plate. Garnish with reserved fennel fronds, if desired. Serve warm or at room temperature, cut into wedges.

Flank Steak Tagliata with Arugula and Parmesan

1 lemon, halved crosswise, divided

3 tablespoons (45 ml) extra-virgin olive oil, divided

4 garlic cloves, grated or minced

1 tablespoon (3 g) chopped fresh rosemary leaves

Kosher salt

Freshly ground black pepper

1 (1½- to 2-pound, or 680 to 908 g) flank steak

5 ounces (about 5 packed cups; 142 g) arugula

Freshly shaved Parmesan cheese, for serving

—

Serves 4 to 6

Maybe it's a holdover from my years as a vegetarian, but my steak cravings are generally few and far between. When I am in the mood, however, this is how I want to eat it. Tagliata is a classic Tuscan preparation of sliced steak most often served over arugula, as it is here. The arugula is the perfect foil for the meat, its spicy freshness cutting through the meat's richness. This is the ultimate make-ahead dinner because the steak can be marinated in the mixture of garlic, rosemary, lemon juice, and olive oil up to 24 hours in advance—though if you have less foresight, it's ready to go after an hour, too.

Squeeze the juice of one lemon half into a shallow dish or zip-top bag large enough to hold the steak. Add 2 tablespoons (30 ml) of olive oil, the garlic, rosemary, 1 teaspoon of salt, and several grinds of black pepper and mix well to combine.

Add the flank steak and coat well in the marinade, using your hands to rub it into the meat—you won't have much excess marinade and that's okay. Cover the steak or seal the bag and refrigerate for at least 1 hour and up to 24 hours.

When ready to cook, place a rack in the top third of the oven. Place a large cast iron skillet or a roasting pan large enough to hold the steak on the rack and preheat the oven to 450°F (230°C). As the oven preheats, take the steak out of the refrigerator to take off some of the chill. The skillet should be in the oven for about 30 minutes (including the time it takes to preheat the oven) before cooking the steak.

Continues >

Continued

Remove the steak from the marinade, carefully place it in the hot skillet, and return the skillet to the oven. Cook for 5 minutes, flip the steak, then continue to cook until nicely browned and firm, 2 to 4 minutes more. An instant-read thermometer inserted into the thickest part of the steak should read 115°F to 120°F (46°C to 49°C) for a rare steak, 120°F to 125°F (49°C to 51.5°C) for a medium-rare steak, and 130°F to 135°F (54°C to 57°C) for a medium steak.

Transfer the steak to a cutting board and let rest for 10 minutes.

Meanwhile, in a large bowl, combine the remaining 1 tablespoon of olive oil and juice from the remaining lemon half with a pinch of salt. Add the arugula and toss to coat. Spread the dressed arugula on a serving platter, leaving room in the center for the steak.

Thinly slice the steak against the grain and arrange the pieces in the center of the platter (it's okay if some of the meat is laying on top of the arugula). Top the arugula and sliced steak with plenty of shaved Parmesan, as well as a few grinds of black pepper, and serve.

Note:

If you look up the proper internal temperature of cooked steak, these suggested temperatures may look a few degrees off to you. That's because the steak will continue to cook off the heat while it rests, so you actually want to pull it 5°F to 10°F (3°C to 6°FC) before your desired doneness.

Broiled Swordfish with Fennel-Caper Slaw

4 tablespoons (60 ml) extra-virgin olive oil, divided

Juice of 1 lemon

2 teaspoons capers, chopped if large (rinsed well if salt-packed)

1 teaspoon Dijon mustard

Kosher salt

Freshly ground black pepper

1 medium fennel bulb, trimmed, quartered, and very thinly sliced with a mandoline or knife (reserve a handful of chopped fronds)

1 tablespoon (3 g) chopped fresh mint

4 (6-ounce, or 170 g) swordfish steaks (about 1 inch, or 2.5 cm, thick)

—

Serves 4

As a kid, everything about coleslaw turned me off: Its stark white color, goopy mayo-laden texture, and how it always seemed to be served ice-cold. Only as an adult did I realize this type of slaw, often bought it tubs in the deli section of the grocery store, is just one interpretation of what slaw can be. Once I lost the mayo and the strict allegiance to cabbage, slaw started making a regular appearance in my life. This unconventional version, made with shaved fennel, capers, lemon juice, and mint, is zippy, fresh, and the absolute perfect complement to broiled swordfish steaks.

In a large bowl, whisk 3 tablespoons (45 ml) of olive oil, the lemon juice, capers, Dijon, ¼ teaspoon of salt, and a few grinds of black pepper to blend. Add the fennel, reserved fronds, and mint and toss to coat. Let marinate at room temperature as you prepare the swordfish.

Place a rack in the top third of the oven (6 to 8 inches, or 15 to 20 cm, from the broiling element) and preheat the broiler to high. Line a rimmed sheet pan with aluminum foil.

Drizzle the remaining 1 tablespoon (15 ml) of olive oil over the swordfish steaks and rub to coat both sides evenly. Season all over with salt and pepper.

Place the swordfish on the prepared baking sheet and broil for 5 minutes. Flip the fish and continue to broil until the fish is opaque, firm, and cooked through, 3 to 5 minutes more. An instant-read thermometer inserted into the middle of the thickest fillet should read 130°F to 140°F (54°C to 60°C).

Toss the slaw once more and serve the swordfish with the slaw piled on top.

Braised Harissa Eggplant and Greens

3 tablespoons (45 ml) extra-virgin olive oil, divided

1 (about 1 pound, or 454 g, total) eggplant cut into ½-inch (1 cm) cubes

Kosher salt

Freshly ground black pepper

1 small yellow onion, finely chopped

3 garlic cloves, minced

1 tablespoon (15 g) harissa, plus more as needed

1 teaspoon ground cumin

2 pounds (908 g) plum tomatoes, or Roma tomatoes, chopped

1 (15-ounce, or 425 g) can chickpeas, drained and rinsed

1 bunch (about 8 ounces, or 227 g) lacinato kale, stemmed, leaves torn into bite-size pieces

1 teaspoon fresh lemon juice

—

Serves 4 to 6

Note:

Enjoy this saucy mess of vegetables and beans over rice, couscous, or quinoa, or simply on its own with good bread.

There's a brief period between summer and fall where it seems that just about every fruit and vegetable is available in abundance at the farmers' market. Although I've long struggled with the transition between seasons, this sweet truth has always made it more tolerable. This stew-like dish celebrates the seasonal overlap when tomatoes are still ruby red, deep purple orbs of eggplant are taut and smooth, and dark, leafy greens arrive in bunches. It's just the thing to make when the weather starts to turn and your craving for cool, crisp salads is replaced by warmer, spicier things. If you're the type that likes to squirrel away good things to uncover in the depths of winter, this is a wise one to double batch and freeze so you can reach for it when nothing but potatoes and onions seem to prevail.

Heat 2 tablespoons (30 ml) of olive oil in a large Dutch oven or heavy-bottomed pot over medium-high heat. Add the eggplant, season with salt and pepper, and cook for about 2 minutes, stirring occasionally, until browned in spots but not completely tender. Transfer the eggplant to a large bowl and set aside.

Reduce the heat to medium and add the remaining 1 tablespoon (15 ml) of olive oil to the pot. Add the onion and sauté until softened and translucent, 3 to 5 minutes. Add the garlic, harissa, cumin, and 1 teaspoon of salt. Sauté until fragrant, about 1 minute.

Stir in the tomatoes, chickpeas, and eggplant and bring the mixture to a simmer. Simmer, uncovered, until the eggplant is meltingly tender and the tomatoes have broken down into a thick, chunky sauce, 25 to 30 minutes.

Stir in the kale and cook until the leaves are bright green and tender, 2 to 3 minutes. Remove from the heat and stir in the lemon juice. Taste and season with additional salt and harissa, as needed, and serve.

Sausage, Pepper, and Onion Oven Bake

3 large bell peppers, assorted colors, cut into 1-inch (2.5 cm) chunks

1 large red onion, cut into 1-inch (2.5 cm) chunks

4 garlic cloves, smashed and peeled

2 tablespoons (30 ml) extra-virgin olive oil

Kosher salt

Freshly ground black pepper

1 pound (454 g) hot Italian sausage, or sweet Italian sausage (chicken, turkey, or pork), casings removed if using links

Coarsely chopped fresh basil leaves, for serving

Freshly grated Parmesan cheese, for serving (optional)

—

Serves 4

On nights when your level of motivation is limited but you still want something warm and satisfying for dinner, let this recipe be your saving grace. Toss a colorful mix of bell peppers and red onion into a baking dish along with smashed garlic cloves and fragrant Italian sausage, and, in about half an hour, you'll have something much greater than the sum of its parts. It's perfect all on its own, topped with chopped basil and grated Parmesan, or it can be tossed with pasta to make it even more substantial, which also stretches it to feed more mouths.

Place a rack in the middle of the oven and preheat the oven to 425°F (220°C).

Place the bell peppers, red onion, and garlic in a 9 × 13-inch (23 × 33 cm) or other 3-quart (3 L) baking dish. Drizzle with the olive oil and season with salt and pepper. Toss to coat and spread into an even layer. Using your hands, break the sausage into large clumps and drop them over the vegetables.

Roast, stirring halfway through, until the sausage is cooked through and the vegetables are tender and lightly caramelized, about 30 minutes. Garnish with basil and serve topped with grated Parmesan, if desired.

Rosemary Brown Butter Scallops

16 (about 1¼ pounds, or 567 g, total) large sea scallops

Kosher salt

Freshly ground black pepper

1 tablespoon (15 ml) extra-virgin olive oil

3 tablespoons (42 g) unsalted butter, cubed

1 tablespoon (3 g) coarsely chopped fresh rosemary leaves

Juice of ½ lemon

—

Serves 4

Scallops have come to have special meaning between my husband, Joe, and me. They're the first thing I cooked for him when we began dating and what he cooked for me the night he proposed. I'll be the first to admit that my preparation so many years ago was overly fussy in an attempt to make him fall for me over my food (though, hey, it did work), but his was so simple, it was arguably much more romantic. We ate these brown butter scallops with sautéed green beans and a bottle of rosé on our tiny apartment balcony before he popped the question. Now, every year on that day, we make the same scallops together, often serving them on a bed of orzo or farro, though you hardly need an occasion to make them yourself.

Pull off and discard the side muscles from the scallops. Pat the scallops dry with paper towels and season with salt and pepper.

Heat the olive oil in a large cast iron or other heavy-bottomed skillet over medium-high heat. Add the scallops and cook, undisturbed, until browned well on the bottom, 3 to 4 minutes.

Turn the scallops, add the butter and rosemary to the skillet, and cook, spooning some of the butter over the scallops, until just cooked through, 2 to 3 minutes. The scallops should be opaque and browned well on both sides. Remove from the heat, drizzle with the lemon juice, and serve.

Skillet Lemon Chicken Thighs with Blistered Olives

4 (about 1½ pounds, or 680 g, total) bone-in, skin-on chicken thighs

Extra-virgin olive oil

Kosher salt

Freshly ground black pepper

½ cup (78 g) Kalamata olives, pitted

1 lemon, halved crosswise, divided

Coarsely chopped fresh parsley, for serving (optional)

—

Serves 4

Like many, once I discovered chicken thighs, it was hard for me to revert to my old boneless, skinless breast ways. They actually taste like something, are basically impossible to cook up to be chalky and tough, and, if you go for the skin-on ones like I usually do, you're rewarded with the browned, crispy results that comes with it. It may seem odd to start the thighs in a cold skillet but doing so actually helps the fat render out of the skin more efficiently so it gets cracker-like crisp. Combined with warm, blistered Kalamata olives and lightly caramelized lemon, it's an easy chicken dinner you'll turn to repeatedly.

Place a rack in the middle of the oven and preheat the oven to 400°F (200°C). Drizzle the chicken thighs with olive oil, rub to coat, and season all over with salt and pepper.

Put the chicken thighs, skin-side down, in a large cast iron or other heavy-bottomed oven-safe skillet and scatter the olives around them. Place the skillet over medium heat and cook, undisturbed, until the skin is browned well and crisp, about 15 minutes.

Cut one lemon half into thin rounds. Remove the seeds from the lemon slices.

Flip the chicken and scatter the lemon slices around it. Transfer the skillet to the oven. Roast until the chicken is cooked through and registers an internal temperature of 165°F (74°C), 8 to 10 minutes.

Squeeze the remaining lemon half over the chicken, sprinkle with parsley, if desired, and serve.

Roasted Cod Saltimbocca

4 (6-ounce, or 170 g) skinless cod fillets (about ¾ inch, or 2 cm, thick), or any firm-fleshed white fish, such as halibut, sea bass, or monkfish

Kosher salt

Freshly ground black pepper

1 tablespoon (15 ml) extra-virgin olive oil

8 fresh sage leaves

4 thin prosciutto slices

Lemon wedges, for serving

—

Serves 4

Saltimbocca *literally translates to "jump in the mouth," as the Italian combination of pungent sage, salty prosciutto, and, usually, veal or chicken does just that. Cod is such a mild fish that its flavor doesn't typically jump in your mouth, so giving it the saltimbocca treatment is hardly a bad idea. This is such a simple way to dress up white fish. It's 100 percent worthy of a gathering with friends, though seeing it's on your table in under 30 minutes, its quickness means it's perfect for harried weeknights, too.*

Place a rack in the middle of the oven and preheat the oven to 400°F (200°C). Pat the fish dry with a paper towel and generously season it all over with salt and pepper.

Pour the olive oil into a baking dish large enough to fit the fillets in one layer and tilt the dish to coat.

Place 2 sage leaves on top of each fillet. Wrap 1 prosciutto slice around each fillet, tucking the ends underneath, and place the fillets in the prepared baking dish.

Roast until the fish is opaque and flakes easily with a fork, 15 to 20 minutes. Serve with lemon wedges for squeezing.

Crispy Spiced Lamb and Cauliflower with Dates

1 lemon, halved crosswise, divided

2 tablespoons (28 g) tahini

2 tablespoons (30 ml) water, divided

Kosher salt

2 tablespoons (30 ml) extra-virgin olive oil

8 ounces (227 g) ground lamb

Freshly ground black pepper

1 large (about 2 pounds, or 908 g, total) head cauliflower, cut into bite-size florets

1½ teaspoons ground cumin

½ teaspoon ground coriander

¼ teaspoon ground cinnamon

¼ teaspoon red pepper flakes

6 Medjool dates, pitted and coarsely chopped

2 garlic cloves, minced

2 tablespoons (6 g) chopped fresh mint

2 tablespoons (17 g) toasted pine nuts, for serving (optional)

—

Serves 4

This dish is a study in how joining ingredients with such stark contrast can result in something surprisingly fabulous. Crispy bits of ground lamb seamlessly meld with tender, seared cauliflower florets and caramelized dates when a healthy hand of warm spices is involved. A lemony tahini sauce drizzled over the whole mess lends a nutty, creamy element that also helps tie things together. Although the pine nuts are optional, given they usually don't come cheap at the grocery store, they do add one more element—a buttery, crunchy one—to this showstopper, so it's worth the splurge, if you're willing.

Squeeze the juice of one lemon half into a small bowl and whisk in the tahini, 1 tablespoon (15 ml) of water, and a pinch of salt until lightened in color and creamy. Add the remaining 1 tablespoon (15 ml) of water and whisk until smooth and pourable. (The mixture may seize up at any point while you add the water, but this is normal. Just keep whisking and it will smooth out.) Set aside.

Heat the olive oil in a large cast iron or other heavy-bottomed skillet over medium-high heat. Add the ground lamb, season with salt and pepper, and cook, breaking up the meat into small pieces with a wooden spoon, until browned and cooked through, 5 to 7 minutes. Transfer to a paper towel–lined plate.

Add the cauliflower to the skillet in a single layer, season with ½ teaspoon of salt and several grinds of black pepper and cook, undisturbed, until the bottoms are browned well.

Reduce the heat to medium and stir in the cumin, coriander, cinnamon, and red pepper flakes. Continue cooking, stirring occasionally, until the cauliflower has developed dark seared spots all over and is tender, 10 to 15 minutes more.

Return the lamb to the skillet and stir in the dates and garlic. Cook, stirring occasionally, until the dates are softened and lightly caramelized, 2 to 3 minutes. Remove from the heat.

Squeeze the remaining lemon half into the skillet, add half of the mint, and lightly toss to combine. Drizzle with the tahini sauce. Serve garnished with remaining mint and toasted pine nuts, if desired.

Baked Chicken Milanese with Lemony Escarole

For Chicken:

2 tablespoons (30 ml) extra-virgin olive oil

2 cups (108 g) Freezer Bread Crumbs (page 23), or panko bread crumbs

Kosher salt

Freshly ground black pepper

1½ pounds (4 medium or 2 large; 680 g) boneless, skinless chicken breasts

2 tablespoons (30 g) Dijon mustard

For Lemony Escarole:

1 bunch (about 12 ounces, or 340 g) escarole

2 tablespoons (30 ml) olive oil

Juice of ½ lemon

Kosher salt

Freshly ground black pepper

Freshly shaved Pecorino Romano cheese, for serving

—

Serves 4

I've always kind of thought of chicken Milanese as sort of an upside-down salad: Crispy chicken piled high with simply dressed greens. Here, the greens are escarole, which have all the crunch romaine lettuce delivers but with a nutty, mildly bitter flavor that plays well with the breaded chicken, lemony vinaigrette, and salty shaved cheese.

—

There are a few tricks to making baked breaded chicken come out as crispy as it would be if fried. First, toast the bread crumbs before dredging the chicken breasts in them. This gives you a jumpstart on browning, so the crumbs won't have to rely completely on the oven to turn them golden. Second, grab a wire cooling rack—the one you use to cool cookies on—and nestle it into your rimmed sheet pan before placing the breaded chicken on top. Baking the chicken on the rack allows air to circulate all around it, so the bottom won't turn soggy.

To make the chicken: Place a rack in the middle of the oven and preheat the oven to 425°F (220°C). Fit a wire cooling rack into a rimmed sheet pan.

Heat the olive oil in a large skillet over medium heat. Add the bread crumbs and toast, stirring frequently so they cook evenly, until golden brown, 7 to 9 minutes. Season with a pinch of salt and a few grinds of black pepper. Remove from the heat and let the bread crumbs cool in the skillet while you prepare the chicken.

If using 4 medium chicken breasts, place one at a time inside a gallon-size zip-top bag and pound with a rolling pin or the flat side of a meat mallet to an even ½ inch (1 cm) thickness. Set aside and repeat with the remaining breasts. If using 2 large chicken breasts, place them on a cutting board and, working with one at a time, lightly press down on the breast with the palm of one hand and use a sharp knife to cut it in half horizontally to make 2 thin cutlets. Repeat with the remaining breast.

Thoroughly pat dry the 4 thin pieces of chicken with paper towels and season all over with salt and pepper. Divide the Dijon among the chicken pieces and use your hands to coat both sides evenly. Dredge each in the toasted bread crumbs right in the skillet off the heat, coating both sides and pressing into the crumbs to adhere. Transfer the coated chicken to the rack on the prepared baking sheet as you go.

Bake until the chicken is cooked through and registers 165°F (74°C) on an instant-read thermometer, 20 to 30 minutes.

To make the escarole: While the chicken bakes, remove and discard any tough outer dark green leaves and halve the escarole lengthwise. Reserve the outer leaves and half of the escarole for another use.

Tear the remaining half into bite-size pieces. You should have about 3 packed cups (100 g).

In a large bowl, whisk the olive oil, lemon juice, a pinch of salt, and several grinds of black pepper to combine. Add the escarole and toss to coat in the vinaigrette. Set aside.

Once the chicken is cooked, transfer it to individual serving plates. Divide the escarole among the plates, piling it on top of the chicken, and top with shaved Pecorino and a few grinds of black pepper.

Note:

What to do with the reserved escarole? Save those tough outer leaves and the remaining half bunch to make sautéed greens tomorrow! Tear or cut the greens into large pieces. Heat a generous drizzle of olive oil in a skillet over medium heat. Add 1 sliced garlic clove, sauté for a minute or two until fragrant but not browned, then add the escarole and season with salt and, if you like, a pinch of red pepper flakes. Sauté for a few minutes until just wilted and tender, then finish with a big squeeze of lemon juice.

Mussels all'Amatriciana

1 (28-ounce, or 794 g) can whole peeled tomatoes

1 tablespoon (15 ml) extra-virgin olive oil

4 ounces (113 g) pancetta, diced

1 medium yellow onion, finely chopped

½ teaspoon red pepper flakes

½ cup (120 ml) dry white wine

4 pounds (1.8 kg) mussels, debearded and scrubbed

Coarsely chopped fresh parsley, for serving

4 thick slices good sourdough bread, or country-style bread, toasted, for serving (optional)

———

Serves 4

If you're never cooked mussels, you'll likely be as shocked as I was the first time I went to buy them at the fish counter: They're so inexpensive! You'll easily find a 2-pound (908 g) bag, which heartily serves two adults, for under $10. Better yet, mussels are just about the fastest, easiest thing you can prepare in your kitchen. Once you discover these two truths, you'll probably never be able to justify paying $20 or more for a pot of them at a restaurant ever again.

———

This recipe is inspired by one of my favorite pastas: pasta all'Amatriciana. The classic dish hails from the small town of Amatrice, about an hour outside of Rome, though it's become equally famous in Italy's capital. Sweet tomatoes, salty pork, and hot red pepper flakes form the base of a savory sauce that these mussels are happy to swim in. Although optional, try not to sleep on serving them with a side of toasted bread because there's lots of good stuff to sop up here.

Empty the canned tomatoes with their juices into a large bowl and carefully crush them with hands (you'll have some bite-size pieces remaining). Set aside.

Heat the olive oil in a large Dutch oven or other heavy-bottomed pot over medium heat. Add the pancetta and cook, stirring occasionally, until it begins to brown and most of the fat has rendered, 4 to 5 minutes. Add the onion and red pepper flakes and sauté until the onion is softened and translucent, 3 to 4 minutes. Carefully stir in the crushed tomatoes and wine. Bring to a simmer and cook, uncovered, for about 5 minutes to allow the flavors to meld.

Add the mussels to the pot and cover it. Cook, shaking the pot vigorously once or twice with the lid still on to distribute the mussels, until the mussels just open, 5 to 8 minutes. Start checking the mussels at 5 minutes, transferring them as they open into individual shallow serving bowls. Discard any mussels that do not open.

Divide the sauce among bowls, spooning the sauce over and around the mussels. Sprinkle with parsley and serve with toasted bread, if desired.

Shawarma-Spiced Halloumi and Vegetables

1 (8.8-ounce, or 250 g) package halloumi cheese, cut into 1-inch (2.5 cm) cubes

2 (about 1 pound, or 454 g, total) sweet potatoes, cut into 1-inch (2.5 cm) chunks

1 pint (about 2 cups, or 300 g) cherry tomatoes, or grape tomatoes

1 small red onion, cut into 1-inch (2.5 cm) chunks

4 garlic cloves, smashed and peeled

1½ teaspoons ground cumin

1 teaspoon paprika

½ teaspoon ground turmeric

¼ teaspoon ground cinnamon

½ teaspoon kosher salt

Freshly ground black pepper

2 tablespoons (30 ml) extra-virgin olive oil

¼ cup (10 g) loosely packed chopped fresh cilantro

———

Serves 4

Some of my favorite dinners are the ones that can seamlessly transition to lunch leftovers. And though you may argue that's most dinners, I say otherwise. A childhood full of microwaved leftovers caused me to be picky: I hate the muted flavor and mushy texture that come with so many. However, make a recipe so bright and bold with flavors and textures, like this one, and it's impossible for it to be dimmed after being tossed in the refrigerator and later carried to the office. The spice mixture of cumin, paprika, turmeric, and cinnamon is heady and warming both straight out of the oven for dinner or served the next day at room temperature. And what's best is, it's truly a one-pan meal—thanks to the protein the salty halloumi cheese brings that intermingles with the vegetables.

Place a rack in the middle of the oven and preheat the oven to 425°F (220°C). Line a rimmed sheet pan with parchment paper. Set aside.

In a large bowl, combine the halloumi, sweet potatoes, tomatoes, red onion, garlic, cumin, paprika, turmeric, cinnamon, salt, and several grinds of black pepper. Toss well to coat the cheese and vegetables in the spices. Drizzle with olive oil and toss to combine. Spread the mixture evenly on the prepared baking sheet.

Roast, gently stirring halfway through, until the halloumi has softened and browned and the vegetables are tender and caramelized, 35 to 40 minutes.

Let the halloumi and vegetables cool for a few minutes. Sprinkle the cilantro over the top, gently toss to combine, and serve.

Eggs in Purgatory

1 (28-ounce, or 794 g) can whole peeled tomatoes

2 tablespoons (30 ml) olive oil

1 small yellow onion, finely chopped

3 garlic cloves, thinly sliced

2 tablespoons (32 g) tomato paste

½ teaspoon red pepper flakes

½ teaspoon kosher salt

Freshly ground black pepper

4 large eggs

¼ cup (10 g) loosely packed coarsely chopped fresh basil leaves

2 ounces (55 g) goat cheese, crumbled (about ½ cup)

Good bread, for serving (optional)

—

Serves 4

If you're familiar with shakshuka—the Middle Eastern dish of eggs poached in tomato sauce—this is the Italian version. The dishes are actually quite similar, especially in the fact that no two recipes are alike aside from all of them containing an aromatic sauce and eggs. My take is heavy on garlic and delivers just the right amount of fire—as the name suggests—even though the origins of the name are unclear. Crumbling goat cheese on top helps tame the heat, as does the soft-cooked runny egg yolks that break when you slice into them. It's definitely my favorite way to eat eggs for dinner.

Empty the canned tomatoes with their juices into a large bowl and carefully crush them with hands (you'll have some bite-size pieces remaining). Set aside.

Heat the olive oil in a large skillet over medium heat. Add the onion and sauté until softened and translucent, 3 to 5 minutes. Add the garlic, tomato paste, and red pepper flakes. Sauté until fragrant and the tomato paste has slightly darkened in color, about 1 minute.

Carefully pour the crushed tomatoes into the skillet, stir in the salt and a few grinds of black pepper, and bring the mixture to a simmer. Gently simmer, uncovered, until the sauce has thickened slightly, about 10 minutes. Remove the skillet from the heat.

Using the back of a spoon, make 4 small wells in the sauce. Crack 1 egg directly into each well.

Gently spoon some of the sauce over some of the egg whites, leaving the yolks exposed (this helps the whites cook faster so they set before the yolks). Cover the skillet and place it over medium-low heat.

Cook, lifting the lid occasionally to check the progress, until the whites are set and the yolks are cooked to your desired doneness, 8 to 12 minutes. The eggs should still jiggle a bit in the centers when you gently shake the pan. Remove from the heat. Sprinkle with goat cheese and basil and serve with bread, if desired.

Broccoli Steaks with Walnut-Raisin Salsa

2 heads (about 1 pound, or 454 g total) broccoli

4 tablespoons (60 ml) olive oil, divided

Kosher salt

Freshly ground black pepper

2 tablespoons (30 ml) sherry vinegar

¼ cup (40 g) golden raisins

½ cup (56 g) walnuts, toasted and chopped

3 ounces (85 g) ricotta salata, crumbled (about ¾ cup)

2 tablespoons (5 g) chopped fresh parsley

1 small garlic clove, grated or minced

Pinch red pepper flakes

—

Serves 4

Notes:

If you can't find ricotta salata, use a firm block of feta cheese.

You may not use all the salsa, but that's hardly a problem—it will keep for a few days in the fridge. Pile what's left on toast, eat it with pita chips, sprinkle it on salads or other roasted vegetables, or spoon it over grilled chicken or steak.

Broccoli rarely gets to play main course, but I've always found it hearty enough to do so. It just needs a little something extra—not much, though—to make it feel like more than a side dish. Let's be honest—cheese always helps. Here, crumbly ricotta salata is the base for a salsa of sorts that's generously spooned over thick, steak-like pieces of roasted broccoli. Added to the cheese are vinegar-soaked raisins, toasted walnuts, herbs, garlic, and red pepper flakes. The result is something that's salty, tangy, sweet, savory, and spicy all at the same time, forcing your taste buds to try to keep up.

Place a rack in the middle of the oven and preheat the oven to 450°F (230°C).

Trim off about ¼ inch (0.6 cm) from the bottom of the broccoli stems to remove their dried ends and use a vegetable peeler to peel away the tough, fibrous skin on the outside of the stems to reveal the pale green flesh. Halve each broccoli head from the stem end lengthwise to get 4 halves and place them on a rimmed sheet pan. Drizzle with 2 tablespoons (30 ml) of olive oil and toss gently to coat, rubbing the oil onto the stems. Lightly season all over with salt and pepper. Place the halves, cut-side down, on the pan and roast until browned and caramelized underneath, 25 to 30 minutes. Flip the broccoli and continue to roast until tender, 10 to 15 minutes more.

Meanwhile, prepare the salsa. In a medium bowl, combine the vinegar and raisins and let rest for 5 minutes to allow the raisins to plump and soften. Add the remaining 2 tablespoons (30 ml) of olive oil, the walnuts, ricotta salata, parsley, garlic, and red pepper flakes. Mix well.

Transfer the roasted broccoli steaks to a serving platter or individual plates. Spoon the salsa generously over the top and serve.

CHAPTER 7

Desserts

My approach to dessert is fairly simple: Enjoy it. I say that as someone with an unyielding sweet tooth who also believes strongly in an everything-in-moderation approach. Satisfying a craving for a slice of cake is just as important as loading your plate with colorful vegetables, if only for your personal well-being. My favorite desserts are the most uncomplicated—those that can be pulled together with only a handful of ingredients. If it's a dessert involving peak-season fruit (as many of my favorites do), this allows their sweetness to really shine. Even if it involves chocolate instead, it means it's something that's easy enough to enjoy without the need for an occasion, because I firmly believe you don't need one.

Chocolate Olive Oil Cake

Ridiculously moist and plush olive oil cake is hard to compete with. In fact, I adore it so much, it was our wedding cake. Although the more classic citrus-kissed version has almost always been my preference (and what we served), there are moments when only something involving chocolate will do. This twist is full of deep, dark chocolate flavor, but what makes this cake stand out from countless other chocolate cakes are the delicate savory notes that come through thanks to the olive oil. It comes together in minutes in a single bowl with pantry ingredients and results in something that ends up feeling pretty special—making it perfect for both celebratory and last-minute cake cravings. Serving a simple chocolate cake like this with freshly whipped cream is nonnegotiable, in my opinion—so is the scattering of crunchy toasted hazelnuts.

¾ cup (65 g) unsweetened cocoa powder, natural or Dutch-process

1 cup (200 g) granulated sugar

½ teaspoon kosher salt

¼ teaspoon baking powder

¼ teaspoon baking soda

¾ cup (180 ml) extra-virgin olive oil, plus more for coating the pan

3 large eggs

1 large egg yolk

1 teaspoon vanilla extract

½ cup (64 g) all-purpose flour

½ cup (120 ml) boiling water

Freshly whipped cream, for serving

Chopped toasted hazelnuts, for serving

—

Serves 8 to 12

Note:

I find that this cake evolves overnight, once the crumb has had even more time to draw out the flavor of the olive oil, resulting in greater flavor depth. So, in the name of science, hold onto a few slices to see how they change. You may even find you prefer the cake after a night's rest, which means it can be a make-ahead dessert the next time you go about baking it.

Place a rack in the middle of the oven and preheat the oven to 325°F (170°C).

Line the bottom of a 9-inch (23 cm) springform pan or an 8- or 9-inch (20 or 23 cm) cake pan with parchment paper. Coat the paper and sides of the pan with olive oil. Set aside.

In a large bowl, whisk the cocoa powder, sugar, salt, baking powder, and baking soda, breaking up any large clumps of cocoa powder, until combined.

Add the olive oil, eggs, egg yolk, and vanilla. Whisk to combine. Add the flour and stir with a rubber spatula until the batter is almost smooth with just a few small lumps; do not overmix. Mix in the boiling water. Pour the batter into the prepared pan.

Bake until the edges of the cake have begun to pull away from the sides of the pan and a tester inserted into the middle comes out clean with just a few crumbs, 25 to 35 minutes.

Transfer the cake in its pan to a cooling rack and let cool for 10 minutes before removing it from the pan. Run a knife around the cake to loosen it. If using a springform pan, unclasp the sides. Otherwise, flip the cake onto a plate, peel away the parchment, and flip it back onto the rack or serving plate.

Serve slices warm or at room temperature, topped with whipped cream and hazelnuts.

Rosé-Soaked Peaches

2 tablespoons (25 g) granulated
sugar

1 teaspoon fresh thyme leaves

2 cups (480 ml) dry rosé wine

4 (about 1¼ pounds, or 567 g,
total) peaches, pitted and cut
into ½-inch (1 cm) wedges

—

Serves 4 to 6

This dessert is about as low effort as you can get, which is useful seeing as peak peach season tends to be the hottest, stickiest time of year, when exerting too much effort is never ideal. Though I'll happily eat the stone fruit straight out of hand, I am all about a fast and fancy way to really show it off. Let peach wedges bathe in wine that's been lightly sweetened with thyme-scented sugar and they become a bit like the fruit at the bottom of a pitcher of sangria—boozy and extra juicy. It's a recipe that's meant to work with your schedule. Let the peaches soak for as little as 2 hours, or up to a whole day, depending on how much time you have.

Place the sugar and thyme leaves in a large bowl. Rub the thyme into the sugar to release its oils. Add the wine and stir until the sugar is dissolved.

Add the peaches and gently toss. Cover and refrigerate for at least 2 hours and up to 24 hours.

To serve, spoon the peaches into small glasses or bowls and drizzle with a few generous spoonfuls of the liquid from the bowl.

Note:

There's no need to use a fancy wine here. Just reach for something you like to drink.

London Fog Affogato

8 scoops vanilla ice cream, or vanilla gelato

¾ cup (180 ml) boiling water

1 Earl Grey tea bag

½ teaspoon dried food-grade lavender buds (optional)

—

Serves 4

I only recently discovered the London Fog latte and quickly fell hard for it. The tea latte made with Earl Grey, steamed milk, and sweetened with vanilla syrup pretty much tastes like being wrapped up in the most snuggly blanket. I am not much of a coffee drinker, due to my sad intolerance for a lot of caffeine, so this tea latte has become a go-to. For that same reason, I rarely enjoy a classic Italian affogato—the simple dessert of espresso poured over vanilla gelato—unless I make it at home with decaf (I know…). This twist on the classic is an ode to my new favorite drink. The citrusy bergamot notes from Earl Grey tea pair so well with vanilla ice cream. Tossing a bit of dried lavender buds (available at spice stores and, sometimes, farmers' markets—just be sure to use "food-grade") into the tea as it steeps adds a delicate floral component that really makes this simple dessert special, but it's totally optional, and the dessert is equally as comforting without it.

Divide the ice cream among 4 serving bowls, glasses, or mugs. Place them in the freezer while you brew the tea.

In a glass measuring cup or teapot, combine the boiling water, tea bag, and lavender (if using). Let steep for 5 minutes. Discard the tea bag, and if using the lavender, strain the tea.

Remove the bowls of ice cream from the freezer. Divide the tea among the bowls, pouring it over the ice cream. Serve immediately.

Apricot Almond Clafoutis

Unsalted butter, for greasing the pan

3 large eggs

⅓ cup (67 g) granulated sugar

1 cup (240 ml) whole milk

¼ cup (32 g) all-purpose flour

¼ cup (25 g) almond flour

½ teaspoon vanilla extract

¼ teaspoon kosher salt

12 ounces (340 g) apricots (about 6), halved and pitted

¼ cup (23 g) sliced almonds

Powdered sugar, for dusting

Freshly whipped cream, for serving (optional)

—

Serves 6

Note:

Sliced peaches make a great substitute if you can't find apricots, as are nectarines and plums. Or try a couple handfuls of blackberries, raspberries, blueberries, halved strawberries, or pitted cherries.

If you can make pancakes, you can make clafoutis. The classic French dessert is no more than a simple egg-rich batter filled with fruit and baked into something that's both custardy and cake-like. Although cherries are most traditional, just about any fresh fruit is made better when turned into clafoutis. I particularly love featuring sweet and tart apricots when they come around because their short season deserves special attention. Apricots pair especially well with almonds—inside their pits are seeds called kernels that actually have an almond-like flavor, which is often extracted and used as a flavoring agent in desserts and liqueurs in France. Rather than have you break out a nutcracker, almond flour and a scattering of sliced almonds lend the complementary notes.

Place a rack in the middle of the oven and preheat the oven to 375°F (190°C). Generously coat an 8- to 10-inch (20 to 25 cm) cast iron or other ovenproof skillet or baking dish with butter and set aside.

In a large bowl, lightly whisk the eggs and sugar. Add the milk, both flours, vanilla, and salt. Whisk to combine, breaking up any large lumps (a few small lumps in the batter are fine). Alternatively, place these ingredients in a blender or food processor fitted with the blade attachment and process until smooth, about 15 seconds.

Arrange the apricot halves in a single layer in the prepared pan. Pour the batter evenly around the fruit, then sprinkle the almonds on top.

Bake until the clafoutis is set, puffed, and light golden brown around the edges, 30 to 35 minutes. Place the skillet on a wire rack and let cool for at least 10 minutes. Serve warm or at room temperature, dusted with powdered sugar and garnished with whipped cream, if desired.

Tahini Truffles

4 ounces (113 g) bittersweet chocolate, or dark chocolate, coarsely chopped (60 to 70% cacao)

½ cup (115 g) tahini, well stirred

¼ teaspoon ground cinnamon

⅛ teaspoon kosher salt

¼ cup (21 g) good-quality unsweetened cocoa powder, natural or Dutch-process

—

Makes 12

Don't let these truffles deceive you. Although they look innocent, they're easily the richest, most decadent recipe in this whole book. If these truffles don't curb a chocolate craving, I am honestly not sure what will. They're so deep and dark and chocolate-y that just one will likely satisfy. Though traditional truffles are made with chocolate and cream, here the cream is replaced with tahini, which is a surprisingly perfect complement. Its savory, nutty notes pair with chocolate much like peanut butter does. Oh, and though there's no wrong way to enjoy them, I will say they go quite well with the last sips of red wine after dinner.

Melt the chocolate in a medium heatproof bowl set over a medium saucepan of barely simmering water, stirring occasionally, until completely smooth. Alternatively, place the chocolate in a microwave-safe bowl and microwave on high power in 30-second intervals, stirring between each, until melted and smooth.

Add the tahini, cinnamon, and salt and whisk to combine. Pour the chocolate mixture into a shallow bowl or baking dish, such as an 8 × 8-inch (20 × 20 cm) baking dish, and refrigerate until firm, about 1 hour.

Once firm, scoop the mixture by the tablespoon and roll into 1-inch (2.5 cm) balls between your hands (friendly warning—your hands will get messy!). Transfer the truffles to a plate or baking sheet and refrigerate for 5 minutes.

Pour the cocoa powder into a small bowl. Dip and roll each truffle in the cocoa powder to coat evenly and transfer to a serving plate. Enjoy immediately or cover and refrigerate for up to 1 week. If refrigerated, let sit at room temperature for 10 minutes before serving.

Note:

If you want to really lean into the sesame notes here, roll the truffles in toasted sesame seeds instead.

Raspberry Ricotta Gratin

1 cup (about 8 ounces, or 227 g) high-quality whole milk ricotta

2 cups (about 9 ounces, or 250 g) fresh raspberries

3 tablespoons (40 g) packed light brown sugar, or dark brown sugar

—

Serves 4

This three-ingredient dessert doesn't need much explanation. Cover fresh raspberries in a thick layer of creamy ricotta, sprinkle it with brown sugar, and broil until the top becomes reminiscent of crème brûlée. The berries just begin to release their juices but remain whole, making it easy to scoop them up with bites of warm, sugared ricotta. I love preparing these in individual ramekins so everyone can break through their own caramelized sugar layer, but it's also fun to make it in one larger dish and just hand everyone a spoon. It almost goes without saying that this technique is lovely with any other berry, too.

Remove the ricotta from the refrigerator to take off its chill while you preheat the broiler. Meanwhile, place a rack in the top third of the oven (6 to 8 inches, or 15 to 20 cm, from the broiling element) and preheat the broiler to high.

Spread the raspberries in a shallow 1-quart (1 L) baking dish or divide among 4 (6-ounce, or 180 ml) ramekins. Top with the ricotta and use the back of a spoon or spatula to spread it over the berries carefully, mostly covering them. Sprinkle the brown sugar evenly over the ricotta, breaking up large clumps with your fingers.

Broil, keeping a close eye to prevent burning, until the sugar melts, bubbles, and begins to caramelize, about 5 minutes. Let cool for 5 minutes before serving.

Citrus Polenta Cake

1 cup (2 sticks, or 226 g)
unsalted butter, at room
temperature, plus more for
the pan

2 large oranges, divided

2¼ cups (225 g) almond flour

1 cup (163 g) polenta (coarse-
ground, not instant or quick-
cooking)

1 teaspoon baking powder

½ teaspoon kosher salt

¾ cup (150 g) granulated sugar

3 large eggs

½ teaspoon vanilla extract

1 lemon

2 tablespoons (40 g) honey

Crème fraîche, or whole milk
plain Greek yogurt, for serving

———

Serves 8 to 12

My very favorite cakes are those that feel totally acceptable to eat for breakfast the next morning. This is one such cake. It's just sweet enough and full of bright citrus flavor. A combination of almond flour and polenta not only creates a light, crumbly texture but also makes it naturally gluten free. Poke holes all over the warm cake once it's out of the oven and drizzle warm honey-citrus syrup over it, and the syrup seeps into every crevice, giving it a sticky tenderness that allows the cake to hold up well for days. In fact, I may even argue it's even better the second or third day after it's baked—one more reason leftovers are ideal morning material. I typically serve slices with nothing but a dollop of something creamy and tangy, like crème fraîche or Greek yogurt, but a handful of blueberries or blackberries is also a nice addition when in season.

Place a rack in the middle of the oven and preheat the oven to 350°F (180°C). Line the bottom of a 9-inch (23 cm) springform pan or an 8- or 9-inch (20 or 23 cm) cake pan with parchment paper. Coat the paper and sides of the pan generously with butter. Set aside.

Finely grate the zest of 1 orange into a small bowl. Halve the zested orange and squeeze the juice into the bowl. Set aside.

In a large bowl, whisk the almond flour, polenta, baking powder, and salt to combine. Set aside.

Place the butter and sugar in the bowl of a stand mixer fitted with the paddle attachment. Alternatively, use a large bowl and an electric hand mixer. Beat on medium speed until light and fluffy, about 3 minutes. Using a rubber spatula, scrape down the sides of the bowl.

With the mixer on low, add the eggs one at a time, beating after each addition. Add the vanilla, pour in the reserved orange zest and juice, and beat until just combined. The mixture will look curdled, but that's okay—it will smooth out in the next step.

Scrape down the sides of the bowl again, then fold in the almond flour mixture using the spatula until the batter is almost smooth with just a few small lumps. Do not overmix. Transfer the batter to the prepared pan and smooth into an even layer.

Bake for 25 minutes. Reduce the oven temperature to 325°F (170°C) and continue to bake until the top of the cake is lightly golden brown, the edges have begun to pull away from the sides of the pan, and a tester inserted into the middle comes out clean with just a few crumbs, 8 to 12 minutes more. Transfer the cake in its pan to a wire cooling rack and let it cool slightly while you make the syrup.

To make the syrup, squeeze the juice of the remaining orange and the juice of the lemon into a small saucepan. Stir in the honey and bring to a boil over medium-high heat. Boil until the mixture is just slightly reduced and a bit syrupy, about 5 minutes.

Using a toothpick, poke holes all over the warm cake. Spoon the hot syrup evenly over the top. Let the cake cool completely.

To serve, run a knife around the cake to loosen it and either unclasp the sides of the pan, if using a springform pan, or, if using a cake pan, flip the cake onto a plate, peel away the parchment, and flip it back onto a serving plate. Serve slices topped with a dollop of crème fraîche or Greek yogurt.

Chocolate Pear Crumble

Nothing against apples, but I think they've long forced pears to take a back seat during fall and winter months. The truth is, I actually prefer the latter. Their sweetness is more complex, in my opinion, and I love their soft yet firm texture. There are so many ways to give pears the attention they rightfully deserve, but I think pairing them with chocolate is one of the most celebratory (not to mention crowd-pleasing). Bitter dark chocolate is a wonderful counterpart to the perfumed, sweet fruit—a match that's common in Italian desserts and an adopted favorite. This simple fruit crumble is best served warm to ensure the chunks of chocolate are still melty. I probably don't need to tell you that vanilla ice cream, although technically optional here, is an option that's very much worth taking.

Unsalted butter, for greasing the pan

For Filling:

2 tablespoons (25 g) packed light brown sugar

1 tablespoon (8 g) cornstarch

½ teaspoon ground cinnamon

2 pounds (908 g) firm but ripe pears, such as D'Anjou or Bosc, peeled, cored, and cut into ¼-inch (0.6 cm) slices

2 teaspoons fresh lemon juice

For Topping:

¾ cup (93 g) all-purpose flour

¾ cup (75 g) old-fashioned rolled oats

⅓ cup (70 g) packed light brown sugar

½ teaspoon kosher salt

6 tablespoons (84 g) unsalted butter, at room temperature, cut into cubes

3 ounces (85 g) bittersweet chocolate, or dark chocolate (60 to 70% cacao), coarsely chopped (about ½ cup)

Vanilla ice cream or freshly whipped cream, for serving (optional)

—

Serves 6 to 8

Place a rack in the middle of the oven and preheat the oven to 375°F (190°C). Coat an 8 × 8-inch (20 × 20 cm) or other 2-quart (2 L) baking dish with butter. Set aside.

To make the filling: In a large bowl, whisk the brown sugar, cornstarch, and cinnamon to break up any clumps. Add the pears and lemon juice and gently toss to coat. Transfer the pears to the prepared baking dish and spread into an even layer.

To make the topping: In the now-empty bowl (no need to wipe it out), combine the flour, oats, brown sugar, and salt. Stir to combine. Add the butter cubes to the bowl and, using your hands, mix and squeeze the mixture together until large, heavy crumbs form and no dry spots remain. Stir in the chocolate. Scatter the topping evenly over the fruit mixture, leaving any large clumps intact.

Bake until the fruit juices are bubbling around the edges of the baking dish and the topping is golden and firm to the touch, 35 to 40 minutes. Let cool on a wire rack for at least 10 minutes before serving warm with vanilla ice cream or freshly whipped cream, if desired.

Greek Yogurt Panna Cotta

1 tablespoon (15 ml) water

½ teaspoon powdered unflavored gelatin

½ cup (113 g) whole milk plain Greek yogurt

½ cup (120 ml) heavy cream, or whole milk, divided

2 tablespoons (25 g) granulated sugar

¼ teaspoon vanilla bean paste, or vanilla extract

Topping of choice, for serving (see suggestions following)

—

Serves 2, but multiplies easily

My relationship with panna cotta runs deep. The very first time I cooked for my husband, Joe, a few months into dating, it's what I made for dessert. When I was living in Italy, I made panna cotta so frequently that my friends pretty much expected it to end a meal when they came over. And at our wedding, it's what we served before dancing and cake. The classic Italian dessert is one of my very favorites, if these examples don't make that obvious.

—

What makes panna cotta so perfect is how quickly it can be prepared—and although it does need some time in the fridge to set up, it is the ultimate make-ahead dessert. Make it the night before or the morning of and it's there for you when you need it. Although panna cotta is typically made with just heavy cream, I love swapping some of the cream for Greek yogurt for just a touch of balancing tang. Using whole milk Greek yogurt and heavy cream will give you the richest results, but you can swap in whole milk for the cream, if you prefer, or if that's what you have in the fridge, for results no less satisfying. Topping options also happen to be nearly endless, though my favorites are listed here.

Note:

If you're not familiar with vanilla bean paste, it's a thick mixture of vanilla extract and scraped-out seeds from vanilla pods. That means it delivers the same great flavor as vanilla extract but comes with the added bonus of those pretty little black flecks, which are especially striking in panna cotta. However, if you'd rather not pick up a jar, your usual vanilla extract works perfectly here, too.

Place the water in a small bowl. Sprinkle the gelatin over the water and set aside to soften.

In a medium bowl, whisk the yogurt and ¼ cup (60 ml) of cream to combine. Set aside.

Place the sugar and remaining ¼ cup (60 ml) of cream in a small saucepan. Bring to a simmer over medium-low heat, stirring occasionally, until the sugar is dissolved, 2 to 3 minutes. Remove from the heat.

Add the gelatin mixture to the warm cream and whisk to dissolve. Pour the mixture through a fine-mesh strainer into the bowl of yogurt to catch any undissolved pieces of gelatin. Add the vanilla bean paste and whisk to combine.

Divide the mixture evenly among 2 (6-ounce, or 180 ml) ramekins or similar-size glasses. Cover loosely with plastic wrap and refrigerate for at least 4 hours, or overnight.

When ready to serve, top with your garnish of choice (see page 200).

8 Fast and Fancy Ways to Top Panna Cotta

Half of what I adore about panna cotta is how versatile it is. It's really the little black dress of desserts, in my opinion. How you top it is up to you—I often base that decision on what's in season and what I have on hand. Here are a handful of my most favorite garnishes:

- **Caramel sauce.** *Don't just save it for ice cream. Salted caramel sauce makes panna cotta extra decadent.*

- **Cooked fruit.** *I topped panna cotta with strawberry rhubarb compote the first time I made it, and it's still a favorite. Just about any fruit can be turned into a compote by simmering it on the stove with a splash of water and a bit of sugar until it turns into a chunky sauce. Let it cool before serving.*

- **Fresh fruit.** *When berries or stone fruits are in season, you really can do no better. Sprinkle berries on top as-is and slice or chop stone fruit like peaches and plums.*

- **Honey, maple syrup, or date syrup.** *This panna cotta isn't overly sweet, so honey and maple syrup are both welcomed toppings. Date syrup, which is made from steamed and pressed dates and has toffee and dark brown sugar notes, is another favorite.*

- **Jams and curds.** *A jar of almost-empty jam or lemon curd is the perfect excuse to make panna cotta—and what I often opt for in winter when good fresh fruit is less of an option.*

- **Olive oil.** *A drizzle of good olive oil is a surprising, yet sophisticated, way to finish panna cotta. A pinch of flaky sea salt seals the deal.*

- **Shaved chocolate.** *If dessert isn't dessert without chocolate, shaving a bit of chocolate on top won't steer you wrong.*

- **Toasted nuts.** *I particularly like a sprinkle of toasted nuts with a drizzle of one of the liquid sweeteners listed here. Coarsely chopped walnuts, hazelnuts, pistachios, and pecans are all nice.*

Roasted Figs with Dark Chocolate and Sea Salt

8 dried figs

1 ounce (28 g) dark chocolate (about 70% cacao), broken or cut into 8 pieces

Extra-virgin olive oil

Flaky sea salt

—

Serves 4

This is one of my favorite emergency desserts. Whether that emergency is impromptu dinner guests or that Monday is said and done and something sweet after the kitchen is cleaned up seems well deserved. Keep dried figs and a bar of dark chocolate in your pantry and you can make this at a moment's notice, even though the results are decadent and special—warm and chewy, sweet and salty—every time.

Place a rack in the middle of the oven and preheat the oven to 350°F (180°C).

Slice the figs through the stem but don't cut all the way through. Tuck a piece of chocolate inside and press the fig halves back together. Place the figs in small baking dish and drizzle with olive oil.

Roast until the figs are warmed through and soft and the chocolate has melted, 5 to 7 minutes.

Drizzle with a little more olive oil, sprinkle with flaky sea salt, and serve.

Note:

It doesn't matter which variety of dried figs you use, but try to buy ones that don't look too old and dried out. If they are, plump them in hot water. Just place the figs in a small bowl, bring some water to a boil, then pour it over the figs to cover. Let sit for 5 to 10 minutes, then drain the figs, discarding the liquid, and lightly pat them dry.

Resources

A Few of My Favorite Brands

California Olive Ranch Their Everyday Extra Virgin Olive Oil is what I use, well, every day in the kitchen for cooking and baking. (www.californiaoliveranch.com)

De Cecco When I lived in Italy, I learned that it's this blue box that Italians reach for at the grocery store rather than the other one. I've followed suit ever since. (www.dececco.com)

King Arthur Flour My favorite brand of flour, though the website is full of all sorts of great ingredients such as high-quality cocoa powder and vanilla bean paste. (www.kingarthurflour.com)

Bob's Red Mill My go-to for whole grains such as farro and polenta, as well as chickpea and almond flour. (www.bobsredmill.com)

Soom The Zitelman sisters' tahini is smooth, nutty, and arguably the best you can find. I also love using their date syrup in place of honey or maple syrup in everything from granola to cocktails. (www.soomfoods.com)

NYShuk Leetal and Ron Arazi are some of the nicest people you'll come across, and once you've tasted any of their Middle Eastern spices or condiments, you'll be hooked for life. Their harissa is the only one I'll buy, and their za'atar is a classic example of the spice blend. (www.nyshuk.com)

Rao's Their jarred marinara is a little more expensive than other brands, but it's the closest to homemade I've found and is a great shortcut to keep on hand. (www.raos.com)

Cento These whole canned tomatoes are high-quality certified San Marzano, and you can taste it. Plus, I've been able to find cans for a reasonable price at Trader Joe's. (www.cento.com)

Pomi Another canned tomato brand I trust and reach for frequently. I use the strained tomatoes for pizza sauce. (www.pomi.us.com)

Maille I've tasted quite a lot of Dijon mustards over the years, but Maille's Original and Old Style (AKA whole grain) is my favorite. (www.us.maille.com)

Rancho Gordo If dried beans have always underwhelmed you, the beautiful, heirloom varieties of Rancho Gordo will change your opinion—as will their Black Caviar lentils. (www.ranchogordo.com)

Specialty Stores

Gustiamo An incredible selection of high-quality imported Italian products such as olive oil, dried pasta, salt-packed capers, and even chocolate. (www.gustiamo.com)

Eataly It's truly an experience to visit an Eataly, if you happen to live near one. Otherwise, you'll find a wide selection of Italian ingredients on their website. (www.eataly.com)

Savory Spice Depending on where you live, there may be a store near you, and it's a great resource for spices. Otherwise, Savory Spice's online selection is vast. (www.savoryspiceshop.com)

Sahadi's When I lived a few blocks away from this Brooklyn landmark for Middle Eastern groceries and prepared foods, you'd find me there weekly. Now you can order almost all of the products online. Don't sleep on Sahadi's selection of nuts and olives. (www.sahadis.com)

Kalustyan's I could lose an entire afternoon wandering the aisles of this international specialty foods store in New York City that's truly an institution. It's worth a trip to the city alone to do so yourself. (www.foodsofnations.com)

Astor Wines & Spirits Another New York City institution that can be delivered to your door, it's a great resource when you can't find a certain wine or spirit locally. (www.astorwines.com)

Acknowledgments

I've had to pinch myself quite a number of times over the past couple of years throughout the process of working on this book as seeing one's lifelong aspiration become reality tends to have that effect. I have more than a few people to thank for that.

To Max Sinsheimer, my literary agent: Thank you for seeing something in me from our very first exchange and putting your faith behind my ideas and this book.

To Thom O'Hearn, my editor: Thank you for giving me this opportunity and for putting up with my endless stream of questions and notes.

To Kristin Teig, Catrine Kelty, and Anne Re: This book wouldn't be much of anything without great photography. Thank you for bringing my vision to life.

To my Kitchn colleagues: I feel so lucky to be a part of such a smart team. Thank you for constantly inspiring me and giving me the space to strive to be better.

To the many food folks who have been such an important part of my career journey along the way, but especially Hali Bey Ramdene, David Tamarkin, Mindy Fox, and Nick Fauchald. Thank you all for being both mentors and friends, for often seeing something in me that I couldn't, and for your ever-ready support and guidance.

To my incredible family and friends, particularly those who eagerly chipped in to recipe test: I am not quite sure how I got so fortunate to have such a strong community around me, but I am sure glad I do.

To Dad, you're the reason I understand what hard work and determination is: Thank you for your endless love and for being the best father and friend a girl could ask for. Tara, watching you go after your ambitions has only made me want to run harder toward mine, and I am forever grateful for that. And Mom, you're the one on my shoulder and the voice in my head; I know you'd be so proud.

And finally, to Joe: Without you giving me the push to follow my dreams way back when, I know as a fact I wouldn't be here. You're my tireless dishwasher and taste tester (I sure glad you love pasta as much as I do), but, more importantly, you are my constant. Thank you for your endless encouragement. I truly am the luckiest.

About the Author

Sheela Prakash is a food and wine writer and recipe developer, as well as a registered dietitian. A longtime editor at Kitchn, she has also been on staff at Epicurious and Food52. Her writing and recipes can be found in numerous online and print publications, including Serious Eats, Tasting Table, The Splendid Table, Culture Cheese Magazine, Clean Plates, and Slow Food USA. She received her master's degree from the University of Gastronomic Sciences in Italy and holds Level 2 and Level 3 Awards in Wines from the Wine & Spirit Education Trust.

Photo by Emily Delamate

Index

A

Affogato, London Fog, 186
Almond Clafoutis, Apricot, 188
almond flour, 188, 194–195
Americano, 51
anchovies, 113, 139–140
Any Herb Pesto, 20–21, 137, 148
Apricot Almond Clafoutis, 188
aromatics, 15
artichokes and artichoke hearts, 63–64, 144
arugula, 63–64, 72, 119, 155–157
asparagus, 58, 103
Avocado, Asparagus Salad with Radishes, Snap Peas, and, 58

B

Baked Chicken Milanese with Lemony Escarole, 170–171
Baked Spinach Artichoke Gnudi, 144
baking supplies, 16
balsamic vinegar, 131–132
basil
    Cucumber Tahini Gazpacho with Crispy Spiced Chickpeas, 74
    Eggs in Purgatory, 177
    Fresh Corn and Tomato Risotto, 99
    Lemony Yogurt and Zucchini Linguine, 127
    No-Cook Summer Tomato Pasta, 120
    Quick Sausage Ragù over Polenta, 106
    Spicy Sausage and Rice Soup, 76
    White Bean Ratatouille over Polenta, 108
beans
    Black Lentil Fritters with Lemon-Herb Yogurt, 87–88
    Garlic Parmesan Soup with Greens and Beans, 79–80
    Mediterranean Niçoise Salad, 63–64
    Olive Oil-Braised White Beans, 84
    Smoky White Bean Hummus, 45
    White Bean Ratatouille over Polenta, 108
beef, 155–157
Black Lentil Fritters with Lemon-Herb Yogurt, 87–88
blue cheese, 48, 153–154

Braised Harissa Eggplant and Greens, 161
bread, 18, 65–66, 111–112, 113, 114, 172
Bread Crumbs, Freezer, 23
broccoli, 139–140, 178
Broccoli Rabe and Chickpea Skillet, Spicy, 89
Broiled Swordfish with Fennel-Caper Slaw, 158
Brussels Sprouts and Farro Bake, Cheesy, 93–95
Burrata and Salsa Verde, Tomato Bread with, 114
butter, 131–132, 132, 163

C

Cacio e Pepe Farinata, 42–44
cakes, 182, 194–195
Campari, 51
canned goods, 16
cannellini beans. See white beans
capers, 41, 139–140, 158
Cappelletti Aperitivo, 51
caramel sauce, 200
Caramelized Leek and Fennel Galette with Blue Cheese, 153–154
Caramelized Mushroom Pasta with Crispy Prosciutto, 125–126
cauliflower, 140, 169
cheese, 48. See also individual types
Cheesy Brussels Sprouts and Farro Bake, 93–95
chicken, 148, 164, 170–171
chickpea flour, 42–44, 90–92
chickpeas, 74, 89, 161
Chili Oil, Spicy, 28
chocolate, 182, 190, 197, 200, 202
cilantro, 74, 141–142, 175
Citrus Polenta Cake, 194–195
Cocchi Americano Bianco, 55
cocoa powders, 182, 190
Cod Saltimbocca, Roasted, 166
Corn and Tomato Risotto, Fresh, 99
Couscous Salad with Herbs, Green Olives, and Pistachios, Israeli, 141–142
Creamy Oven Polenta, 105, 106, 107, 108
Crispy Spiced Chickpeas, 74
Crispy Spiced Lamb with Cauliflower and Dates, 169
cucumber, 65–66, 68, 74

D

Dates, Crispy Spiced Lamb with Cauliflower and Dates, 169

E

Easiest Arugula Salad, The, 72
eggplant, 108
eggs, 63–64, 161, 177
escarole, 170–171, 171
Everyday Vinaigrette, 27

F

Farinata, 42–44
farro, 93–95, 95
fennel, 47, 72, 153–154, 158
feta cheese, 70, 90–92, 123, 178
figs, 48, 202
fish and seafood
    Broiled Swordfish with Fennel-Caper Slaw, 158
    Hot Smoked Salmon Greek Salad, 68
    Mussels all'Amatriciana, 172
    Orzo Skillet with Shrimp and Feta, 123
    Pasta with Burst Cherry Tomatoes and Swordfish, 134
    Roasted Cod Saltimbocca, 166
    Rosemary Brown Butter Scallops, 163
    Salmon in Crazy Water, 151
    Shrimp Scampi over Polenta, 107
Flank Steak Tagliata with Arugula and Parmesan, 155–157
flours, 16
focaccia, 111–112, 112
Fontina cheese, 100
Freezer Bread Crumbs, 23, 128–130, 139–140, 170–171
freezer staples, 18
Fresh Corn and Tomato Risotto, 99
fruit, 185, 188, 193, 197, 200

G

Galette with Blue Cheese, Caramelized Leek and Fennel, 153–154
garlic, 30, 39, 79–80
goat cheese, 38, 48, 70, 177
grains, 16

Greek yogurt. *See* yogurt
green beans, 63–64
greens, 79–80, 161
Gruyère cheese, 93–95

H

Halloumi and Vegetables, Shawarma-
  Spiced, 175
Harissa Eggplant and Greens, Braised,
  161
hazelnuts, 71, 93–95, 131–132
Herb-Infused Honey, 50
herbs
  Any Herb Pesto, 20–21
  Black Lentil Fritters with Lemon-
    Herb Yogurt, 87–88
  Herb-Infused Honey, 28
  Herby Ricotta, 34
  Israeli Couscous Salad with Herbs,
    Green Olives, and Pistachios,
    141–142
  Lemon-Herb Yogurt, 87–88
  Peak-Summer Panzanella, 65–66
  Salsa Verde, 25
  See also individual herbs
honey
  Herb-Infused Honey, 28
  Honeyed Prosecco, 50
  as panna cotta topping, 200
Hot Smoked Salmon Greek Salad, 68
Hummus, Smoky White Bean, 45

I

ice cream, 186
Israeli Couscous Salad with Herbs,
  Green Olives, and Pistachios,
  141–142

J

jarred goods, 16

K

kale, 71, 161

L

Lamb with Cauliflower and Dates,
  Crispy Spiced, 169
leeks, 103, 153–154
lemons, 87–88, 103, 127, 164, 170–171

Limonata Smash, 52
London Fog Affogato, 186

M

Mediterranean diet, about, 12
Mediterranean Niçoise Salad, 63–64
Melon and Prosciutto Caprese,
  Mixed, 61
Melted Broccoli Pasta with Capers and
  Anchovies, 139–140
mint, 52
Mixed Melon and Prosciutto Caprese,
  61
mozzarella, 61, 113
muddling, 52
mushrooms, 101, 125–126
Mussels all'Amatriciana, 172

N

No-Cook Summer Tomato Pasta, 120
No-Fail Parmesan Risotto, 96–98
nuts, 36, 71, 93–95, 131–132, 178, 200

O

oils, 15, 28
olive oil, 84, 182
olives
  about, 64
  Hot Smoked Salmon Greek Salad, 68
  Israeli Couscous Salad with Herbs,
    Green Olives, and Pistachios,
    141–142
  Mediterranean Niçoise Salad,
    63–64
  as panna cotta topping, 200
  pitted versus with pits, 39
  Roasted Garlic-Marinated Olives, 39
  Skillet Lemon Chicken Thighs with
    Blistered Olives, 164
Onion Oven Bake, Sausage, Pepper,
  and, 162
oranges, 194–195
Orzo Skillet with Shrimp and Feta, 123

P

panna cotta, 199, 200
pantry enhancers
  about, 19
  Any Herb Pesto, 20–21
  Everyday Vinaigrette, 27

Freezer Bread Crumbs, 23
  Herb-Infused Honey, 28
  Roasted Garlic, 30
  Salsa Verde, 25
  Spicy Chili Oil, 28
pantry staples, 15
Panzanella, Peak-Summer, 65–66
Parmesan cheese
  Baked Spinach Artichoke Gnudi, 144
  Cheesy Brussels Sprouts and Farro
    Bake, 93–95
  Creamy Oven Polenta, 105
  The Easiest Arugula Salad, 72
  Fennel and Parmesan "Crostini," 47
  Flank Steak Tagliata with Arugula
    and Parmesan, 155–157
  Fresh Corn and Tomato Risotto, 99
  Garlic Parmesan Soup with Greens
    and Beans, 79–80
  Lemony Asparagus Risotto, 103
  No-Fail Parmesan Risotto, 96–98
  saving rinds from, 80
  Spaghetti and Meatball Ragù,
    128–130
parsley, 128–130, 134, 141–142
pasta, about, 16
peaches, 185, 188
Peak-Summer Panzanella, 65–66
Pear Crumble, Chocolate, 197
peas, snap, 58
Pecorino Romano cheese, 42–44, 101,
  127
Pepper, and Onion Oven Bake,
  Sausage, 162
pesto, 20–21, 137, 148
pistachios, 36, 141–142
polenta, 105, 106, 107, 108, 194–195
potatoes, 63–64, 148
prosciutto, 48, 61, 125–126, 166
Prosecco, Honeyed, 50

Q

Quick Sausage Ragù over Polenta, 106

R

radicchio, 101, 137
Radishes, Snap Peas, and Avocado,
  Asparagus Salad with, 58
Raisin Salsa, Broccoli Steaks with
  Walnut-, 178
Raspberry Ricotta Gratin, 193

red peppers, 41, 108
refrigerator staples, 18
rice, 76, 96–98, 98, 99, 100, 101, 103
ricotta, 34, 144, 193
ricotta salata cheese, 71, 120, 178
risotto rice, 96–98, 98, 99, 100, 101, 103
Roasted Cod Saltimbocca, 166
Roasted Figs with Dark Chocolate and
    Sea Salt, 202
Roasted Garlic, 30
Roasted Garlic-Marinated Olives, 39
Roasted Greek Tomato Soup, 73
Rosemary Brown Butter Scallops, 163
Rosé-Soaked Peaches, 185

S

Sage Risotto, Sweet Potato and, 100
salmon, 68, 151
Salsa Verde, 25, 114
sausage, 76, 106, 162
scallions, 58
Scallops, Rosemary Brown Butter, 163
seafood. *See* fish and seafood
seasonings, 15
Shawarma-Spiced Halloumi and
    Vegetables, 175
sherry vinegar, 41
shrimp, 107, 123
Skillet Lemon Chicken Thighs with
    Blistered Olives, 164
Slinky Red Peppers with Capers and
    Sherry Vinegar, 41
Smoky White Bean Hummus, 45
Snap Peas, and Avocado, Asparagus
    Salad with Radishes, 58
Spaghetti and Meatball Ragù, 128–130
Spicy Broccoli Rabe and Chickpea
    Skillet, 89
Spicy Chili Oil, 28
Spicy Sausage and Rice Soup, 76
spinach, 131–132, 144
squash, 71, 108, 127
sweet potatoes, 100, 175
swordfish, 134, 158

T

tahini, 74, 169, 190
Thyme Pesto Roasted Chicken with
    Crispy Potatoes, 148
tomatoes
    Braised Harissa Eggplant and
        Greens, 161
    Chickpea Flatbread with Whipped
        Feta and Marinated Tomatoes,
        90–92

Eggs in Purgatory, 177
Fresh Corn and Tomato Risotto, 99
Hot Smoked Salmon Greek Salad, 68
Mediterranean Niçoise Salad,
    63–64
Mussels all'Amatriciana, 172
No-Cook Summer Tomato Pasta,
    120
Orzo Skillet with Shrimp and Feta,
    123
Pasta with Burst Cherry Tomatoes
    and Swordfish, 134
Peak-Summer Panzanella, 65–66
Quick Sausage Ragù over Polenta,
    106
Roasted Greek Tomato Soup, 73
roasting, 73
Salmon in Crazy Water, 151
Shawarma-Spiced Halloumi and
    Vegetables, 175
Spaghetti and Meatball Ragù,
    128–130
Spicy Sausage and Rice Soup, 76
Tomato Bread with Burrata and
    Salsa Verde, 114
White Bean Ratatouille over
    Polenta, 108
Tortellini with Spinach and Hazelnuts,
    Balsamic Brown Butter, 131–132
Truffles, Tahini, 190
tuna, 63–64

V

vanilla beans, 199
vinaigrette, 27, 63–64, 71
vinegars, 15

W

Walnut-Raisin Salsa, Broccoli Steaks
    with, 178
Warm Roasted Delicata Squash and
    Kale Salad, 71
white beans, 45, 79–80, 84, 108
Whole-Wheat Skillet Focaccia,
    111–112, 177

Y

yogurt
    Black Lentil Fritters with Lemon-
        Herb Yogurt, 87–88
    Chickpea Flatbread with Whipped
        Feta and Marinated Tomatoes,
        90–92
    Greek Yogurt Panna Cotta, 199
    Hot Smoked Salmon Greek Salad, 68

Lemon-Herb Yogurt, 87–88
Lemony Yogurt and Zucchini
    Linguine, 127

Z

za'atar, 36, 38
zucchini, 108, 127